W9-BUE-552

INVESTING
for the
FUTURE

INVESTING
for the
FUTURE

Larry Burkett

VICTOR BOOKS ®

A DIVISION OF SCRIPTURE PRESS PUBLICATIONS INC.
USA CANADA ENGLAND

All Scripture quotations are from the *New American Standard Bible,* © the Lockman Foundation 1960, 1962, 1963, 1968, 1971, 1972, 1973, 1975, 1977.

Editor: Greg Clouse

Cover Designer: Paul Higdon

Cover Photo: The Image Bank

Library of Congress Cataloging-in-Publication Data

Burkett, Larry.
    Investing for the future / by Larry Burkett.
      p.   cm.
    Includes bibliographical references.
    ISBN 0-89693-889-1
    1. Investments—United States. 2. Investments—United States—
Moral and ethical aspects. 3. United States—Economic conditions—1981
- I. Title.
HG4910.B86 1992
332.6'0973—dc20   91-27331
                                                   CIP

5 6 7 8 9 10 Printing/Year 96 95 94 93 92

Contents

Introduction

When I was first approached by the editors at Victor Books about writing a book on investing, I declined. My feelings then were the same as now. I am not an investment advisor, nor do I desire to be. A genuine concern I have is that someone might misinterpret what I say and lose some hard-earned money. If that person makes money by investing money it would be bad enough. But many of the people I know make their money by investing their labor. Advising them on how to risk that money is a grave responsibility that I have no desire to assume.

But, as you can tell by now, I decided to write a book on investing. My reason for doing so is that, as a teacher and counselor, I have seen most of the mistakes that can be made with money—including investing. As a result, I believe I can help you to avoid some bad decisions and make some good ones. I hope you will find this book unlike any you have ever read. In reality it is not one book but several related topics put under one cover.

First, it is an overview of the economy and how it affects investment strategy.

Next, it is a basic overview of what God's Word has to say about investing, and the biblical principles of multiplication.

Then it shifts to what I call "the hall of horrors": the investment errors that usually result in the maximum loss for those who choose to risk their resources foolishly. I believe that I have seen virtually every way someone can lose money. The investments may change from time to time, but the same strategies persist.

The next section is dedicated to understanding which investments to use at the different stages of life. This is an age-related study on how to develop sound investment strategies. The goals at each stage (20–40, 40–60, 60+) all differ, but the end result is to become debt-free and develop enough surplus to live comfortably while pleasing the Lord in the process.

The last section evaluates the various investment groups (secure, long-term income, growth, speculation, and high-risk) and places them in a five-tiered strategy to help determine which is best at any stage of life.

I have tried not to duplicate work done by others who have written on this subject where I believe their efforts are valid. Instead I refer to their works in the Appendix as resources for those seeking more in-depth analysis on specific investments.

Investing is anything but an exact science, as anyone who has ever lost money on a "sure thing" can testify. But there are basic rules that apply to investing, just as there are basic rules for physics. For example, the law of gravity says that an object will be drawn toward another object of greater mass. Thus when you jump into the air you ultimately come back down to earth. If you fill a balloon with helium it will seemingly defeat the law of gravity, but only until the helium leaks out; then it will return to earth again.

Investing's law of risk and return works the same way. The higher the promised rate of return, the higher the risk of losing your money. Economic upturns and inflationary markets can temporarily make that law seem defeatable, but eventually the market deflates and the high-return investments plummet to earth again, along with your hard-earned savings.

If you gain but one perspective from this book, I trust it will be this: *The rules from God's Word about investing still work.* Apply them and you will prosper over the long run. Violate them and you will lose all that you have worked so hard to accumulate.

I am grateful to many friends who have contributed their collective knowledge to *Investing for the Future.* Not one of them boasts of never having made an investment mistake. Most will readily admit that they are wrong sometimes and they are right sometimes. The saving feature of their counsel is that they are right more often than they are wrong, and they try to minimize the downside risk while maximizing the gain, so over the long run their clients prosper.

I am especially grateful to one of my best friends, a skilled professional in the field of medicine. It was from him and his colleagues that I learned a valuable insight: It is possible to attain a nearly perfect track record in the area of investments while relying almost exclusively on intuition and the advice of others. How do I know this, you ask? Because he and his colleagues have been nearly 100 percent wrong in every investment they have made. Therefore, if one would simply study the techniques they employ and do the exact opposite, he would come out ahead. It's not always perfect, but it comes pretty close.

I will confess from the outset that I am personally a very conservative investor. I stay with things that have proven their worth over several decades, and try not to vary during good times or bad. The so-called "dollar averaging" approach usually pays off in the long run. If you're not familiar with this technique, you will be by the time you have finished this book.

I also don't want to get up in the morning and have to rush out to buy a copy of *The Wall Street Journal* to see how my investments are doing. I am more than willing to pay someone else a fee to do that for me. In my case, I elect to use good quality mutual funds with professional management. You may prefer to do your own investing, which is totally your choice. What I will try to do is evaluate what the professionals have done so you can decide if you have done better or worse. The bottom line with any financial management fee, regardless of whether it is a financial planner's fee or a fund management fee, is: Can they cover their fees and still do better than you can on your own? If so, it would be silly not to use them. If not, then their service is a waste of money.

The one area of investment counsel that irritates me the most is to have someone present an investment in glowing terms, only to find out later that he didn't reveal the whole truth. Therefore, in this book I will try to be brutally honest. I know this will alienate some Christians who sell investments, but I believe it is preferable to alienate a few salespeople rather than allow more of their clients to lose money because of ignorance.

Good reading, God bless you, and I trust you will decide this book is one of the best investments you have ever made.

1

The Economy

T here is virtually no way to write a book on investing without first discussing the economy. After all, what is an investment except an idea to make money? If that idea is not matched to the economy it is almost certainly doomed to failure. For instance, an investment of $1,000 in the Ford Motor Company in 1912 would have grown to nearly $12 million by 1950. Inflation consumed about half of its buying power during the intervening years, so an investor in Ford was left with a mere $6 million on which to retire. Not a bad deal.

The equivalent investment of $2,000 in 1950 in the same stock would have been worth about $50,000 in 1990. Still not a bad return, except that inflation would have eroded its buying power to about $10,000. Clearly the economy had a major effect on the value of investments made in the early and latter part of the twentieth century.

What might you have done with your $2,000 in 1950 to improve your retirement income? You might have guessed that the world would have a computer revolution in the next 40 years and invested your money in IBM. If you had purchased $2,000 worth of IBM common shares in 1950, your investment would have grown to nearly $700,000 by 1990.

Or you might have chosen a new investment idea called a mutual fund. This is a plan in which many investors pool their assets and invest in a wide spectrum of stocks or bonds. Several of the top funds would have yielded a return of nearly $2 million on your original $2,000.

Or you could have invested in Symmetrics Engineering (as I did in 1959) and watched your stock value go from $2 a share to $30 a share in just four years, only to plummet to zero five years later when the Japanese entered the electronics business.

Now that we have established that the economy has a direct bearing on which investments do well or poorly, I would like to give a short refresher course on how our economy operates.

Prior to the twentieth century our economy operated by what was called monetarist, or free market, economic theory. Simply put, monetarist theory means that the government plays little or no role in determining the direction of the economy. Prior to this century if the economy slumped into a recession (or depression), the government did not feel compelled to step in and bail it out. Nor did the average American expect direct government intervention. After all, if private businesses caused the problems, they should solve the problems, right?

Prior to this century, no Americans drew welfare from the government. No farmers were paid not to grow food. No homes were subsidized by government loans, and the "homeless" who wouldn't work were called "bums." One side benefit of free-market economics was that Americans were allowed to keep 100 percent of what they earned. Taxes were collected through the sale of goods, through tariffs, not income confiscation. Governments ran lean and efficient; because if they didn't, they shut down.

A NEW THEORY OF ECONOMICS

World War I made an indelible impact on this nation. From an isolationist country we emerged with much more of a global mentality. Certainly that was true where economics was concerned. The devastation of Europe presented unparalleled opportunities for Americans to expand their businesses. With the industrial revolution in full swing, American businesses exported automobiles, telephones, food, and technology worldwide.

Unfortunately, what American business schools imported was an idea that had just begun to take root in Europe: socialism. Professor John Maynard Keynes, a British economist, and an avowed socialist, had succeeded in establishing his doctrine of government intervention in private business throughout European academics.

Simply put, Dr. Keynes believed that it was the role of governments to manipulate the economies of their countries so as to lessen the effects of economic cycles. He taught that during good economic times a government should confiscate funds from the economy and use them to promote socially mandated programs such as health care, shelter, jobs, and such: the Robin Hood syndrome, if you will.

Then during economic downturns the government would supply capital as needed to stimulate growth and economic recovery. (The difficulty arises when the social programs expand during bad times and the governments are enticed to borrow to continue their operations.)

In the poorer nations, where the economies were already controlled by the governments, this concept was adopted wholeheartedly, but they lacked the resources to give the theory a platform from which to experiment. So what better place to experiment than in America, where free market economics, based on a biblical heritage, had built the strongest economy in the world with tremendous surpluses available to pilfer.

Keynesian economics swept the world. From it was born the International Monetary Fund and the World Bank. In America came the Federal Reserve system, the federal income tax system, the Social Security system, the Job Corps program, the Farm Bank, the Federal Depositors Insurance Corporation, and on and on it went. The real impetus to adopt Keynesian economics came during the Great Depression of the 1930s. In reality the Great Depression was exacerbated by President Hoover's ill-advised decisions to raise taxes on consumer goods to feed the government's growing need for funds, and the incredibly nearsighted move to establish import quotas on foreign goods, which triggered a worldwide protectionist movement.

Herbert Hoover was booted out of office and Franklin Roosevelt was voted in with a mandate to implement Keynesian economics at every level of government. Adding momentum to these social changes was America's entry into World War II. During this period the checks and balances of the Constitution were suspended in favor of almost dictatorial powers for the president. Coming out of the war the expanded role of the central government grew until it touched the lives of virtually every American.

What we see and accept as normal today would have sparked a revolution in *any* generation prior to this century. When the federal income tax system was first suggested in 1912 it was promoted as a "voluntary" system because the supporters were fearful that the electorate would revolt if the government tried to force compliance. When Congress voted to accept the voluntary tax system, it was argued that a 1.5 percent cap should be placed on what the federal government could raise in income taxes. The resolution was soundly defeated on the basis that Americans would never allow their government to take such large sums from their wages. It was argued that if the Congress approved such a limit some future politician might be tempted to seek that outrageous amount.

From those humble beginnings we have evolved into a full-blown Keynesian-run economy. Nothing happens that does not in some way involve the federal government in everyday business affairs. The average American now believes it is the duty of our government to control the economy.

The difficulty with government manipulation of the economy is that each action creates a greater reaction and requires more manipulation. Lowering interest rates and producing credit out of thin air definitely stimulates the economy. But the laws of supply and demand swing into play, and with more people competing for the available products, prices go up and we have inflation.

When I went to college in the sixties, it was accepted that we could live with an inflation rate of 1 percent a year, and long-term interest rates as high as 4 percent. After all, with an inflation rate of 1 percent it would take 50 years or so for prices to double. And with interest rates at 4 percent your savings would double in just 18 years. No problem—right?

Except that the inflation rate didn't stay at 1 percent. Inflation is a ratio of how much new or unsecured money is put into the economy versus how much real money and assets exist. So as the government created new money out of thin air the ratio changed rapidly. Allow me to use an example.

In 1960, gold (the standard for real value for about 3,000 years) traded for about $35 an ounce on the world market. (Franklin Roosevelt had outlawed the ownership of gold in America in order to create fiat money.) The price for an ounce of gold didn't change significantly until it became legal to own gold in the U.S. again. In the meantime people began to figure out that the United States had printed a lot of new dollars with virtually nothing of any real value to back them up. Gold prices climbed rapidly once it was legal to own it again, and even ignoring the rapid speculative runup in gold prices during the late seventies, gold leveled out at around $350 to $400 an ounce—an increase of about 1,000 percent! Very few fixed-dollar investments kept track with that increase. But gold didn't actually inflate by over 1,000 percent. Gold was merely acting like an inflation barometer, reflecting the inflation that had taken place in our economy. In real buying power, investors holding paper money had lost much of their savings.

One might argue that prices didn't increase by 2,000 percent during the last 30 years, and interest rates increased to help make up some of the inflation.

I would agree (to some extent). Interest rates leveled out in the eighties at around 10 percent a year. At 10 percent, paper money investments doubled about every seven years or so. In fact, interest rates paid to investors really only reached the 10 percent level in the late eighties. But even if the rate had been 10 percent for the 30-year period from 1960 to 1990, an investor's assets would have increased only about 500 percent. That is impressive sounding, but not compared to an inflation increase of 2,000 percent.

What about real assets? An average three-bedroom home in 1960 sold for about $10,000. In 1990 that same home (not a new one—the *same* home) sold for approximately $108,000, yielding an inflation rate of nearly 1,100 percent!

A family-sized Chevrolet sold for about $2,600 in 1960. In 1990 the same (but smaller) model sold for approximately $16,800, an inflation increase of about 650 percent. And on it goes. . . .

The point I am trying to make here is that the economy has a *direct* effect on anyone's investment philosophy, whether we want it to or not. So understanding something about the economy is essential to long-term saving. The shorter the time period, the more difficult it is to project the direction of an economy. What any knowledgeable investor must do is look at trends. Trends often develop over years, not months, and certainly not weeks.

Since this is not a book on economics I won't discuss the background of our economy any further. (For more detail on that subject, I would refer you to my book, *The Coming Economic Earthquake,* Moody Press, 1991.) But it is important to discuss where we seem to be headed. If you believe we are going to have significant long-term inflation, then your long-term investment strategy should be aggressive and diversified. But if you believe the economy will slump into a decade-long depression (as some project), then your strategy should be maximum protection of your capital.

The difficulty is that good arguments can be made for either scenario (and several others). Eventually, you must pick a side and commit yourself. I personally believe that a balanced strategy, where assets are invested in a variety of categories, is the wisest approach.

THE FUTURE ECONOMY

With some degree of certainty I can say that the economy of the nineties, and well into the twenty-first century, will not be like that of the past 40 years. In the fifties we were the world's industrial leader with a huge surplus of trade and very little government debt. It was a wise investor who would borrow at 4 percent and invest in growing businesses that would yield 6 to 12 percent.

The sixties and early seventies was the era of massive debt funding, and by the late seventies inflation was raging and interest rates had soared. Those who borrowed money to make investments found themselves saddled with 20-percent loans in 10-percent investments. Only the incentives of ill-conceived tax shelters enticed the foolish to follow this path.

In the early eighties "Reaganomics" lowered interest rates and income taxes to stimulate a depressed economy. The eighties will surely be known as the era of junk bonds, tax shelters, and huge debts. The legacy of "Reaganomics" is the demise of the savings and loan industry, as well as several hundred banks that engaged in the debt expansion.

The debt bubble has burst and the fallout is still being determined at this time. The nineties will present unparalleled challenges to retirees trying to salvage their life savings from the ravages of a fluctuating economy and plodding inflation. A debt-ridden government gone spending-crazy will turn over every economic rock possible to generate the capital it needs to feed the "system" just a little while longer. Social Security will need huge infusions of capital as the baby boomers approach retirement. The cash reserves that should be held in trust have been spent by the government, and the wage earners of the twenty-first century will be tapped as no generation before them. You can be sure that the eligible voters of the next century will demand reform of the system that would rob them of a reasonable standard of living. Therefore, a prudent investor would do well to look to his own reserves for the retirement years. But we'll discuss that more fully later.

RECESSIONS, DEPRESSIONS, AND RECOVERIES

Almost everyone has a theory about where the economy is headed. There is the depression theory, the inflation theory, the deflationary-inflation theory, the inflationary-depression theory, and so on. I also have an opinion, but I prefer to keep it to myself until later because if you don't hold to my opinion you may get distracted and stop reading.

The one certainty is: The economy won't stop; none ever has. The economy periodically slumps into what is commonly called a recession. A recession is neither mystical nor inexplicable. Generally speaking, a recession is caused by consumers reducing their level of spending from what it was previously. Usually the cycle of comparison is three months. In other words, if consumer spending drops for three consecutive months, the economy is considered to be "in a recession."

Obviously there are several other factors that are measured, such as consumer confidence (whatever that is), durable goods output, the wholesale index, the inventory index, the Federal Reserve index, etc. I'm convinced that most of these are created to employ economists who otherwise would have very little to talk about on the evening news.

The reasons for any economy to suffer through a recession are varied. In our generation the primary cause of recessions is consumers who take on too much debt and then have to cut back on spending to pay it off. The reduction in new debt is reflected in lower sales—hence a recession. Certainly the recession of the early nineties can be traced directly back to the credit binge of the eighties. The same can be said of the larger recession of the mid-seventies.

Recessions occur about every seven to eight years and last from a few months to as long as three years. They rarely affect the entire economy, and seldom encompass the entire country. These economic downturns are called recessions, rather than depressions, primarily because of the depth and breadth of the downturn. In reality, a recession is simply a less severe and more localized depression.

Generally, depressions occur in 50- to 70-year cycles. Again, this is not some mystical timing. It is the normal operation of market cycles. As debt becomes more pronounced in an economy, the prices of goods (land, stocks, buildings, etc.) are bid higher and higher. The shorter recessions relieve the upward pressures somewhat, but often the very thing that helps the economy to recover from a recession—more debt—is what leads to the longer, more severe depression.

Ultimately the economy cannot handle any additional debt as loans have been extended for 30-, 40-, or even 50-year periods. Prices begin speculative runups based on the availability of easy credit, and even the most conservative of investors wants to get in on the action. Suddenly bankers get very nervous when they see loans being maintained through more borrowing and defaults becoming more common, and they pull the plug. Marginal loans get called, borrowers default, and the downward spiral begins.

Usually a depression is not a steep drop into an economic abyss. Instead, it is a series of recessions followed by an increasing abundance of government-sponsored debt to shore up the flagging system. One event can often trigger the collapse. It can be as simple as a sudden drop in stock market values, as in 1929. Or it may be as insidious as the government printing money to pay its bills, as Germany did in 1919, before their great depression.

Eventually the economy will recover; it always does. It may

be altered somewhat and no longer be tied to the gold standard, as happened to the U.S. in the Great Depression. After the next depression (and I do believe there will be another one), we may find that we use no currency at all. Predicting when and how the next depression will occur is almost impossible without a great deal of speculation. One logical projection is the last half of this decade when government debt reaches the $10 *trillion* mark, and the annual deficits reach $1 trillion a year! Depression in a debt-run economy is as certain as death. The question is not "if," but "when."

Again, the point I would like to make here is that the economy *will* recover and, if you can wait it out, so will you. The key to surviving in the short run is to carry as little debt as possible into the downturn, avoid selling when prices are down, and have enough cash on hand to buy good assets when the prices are down. Those who are in debt and in need of quick money to pay the bankers will be the losers because they will be forced to sell regardless of the loss. The economic principle is simple: It's better to be a buyer during a down cycle; then sell when the economy recovers. What is the key principle? *No debt!*

As I close this chapter, I would like to acquaint you with two key facts that should motivate you to watch the economy and make some changes in the way you perceive the future.

1. *The "on-budget" debt of the federal government is rapidly approaching $4 trillion.* "On-budget" refers to the posted amount uncontested by the Washington bureaucrats. The real debt is closer to $8.5 trillion. This includes the funds pilfered from the Social Security trust, deposit guarantees to cover the deficiencies at the savings and loans and banks, projected income deficiencies for federal retirees and service personnel, defunct retirement accounts, and insurance company defaults. There is perhaps another $500 to $600 billion in debt to secure home loans, farm loans, school loans, etc.

2. *By 1996, at the current rate of deficit, it will take all of the taxes paid by all taxpayers to pay the interest on the national debt.*

The federal government will be spending money at the rate of approximately $7 billion per minute! If a husband sent his spouse out to spend a million dollars at the rate of $1,000 per day, she would return in about three years. If he sent her out to spend a billion dollars at the same rate, she would return in about 3,000 years.

WHY THE U.S. ECONOMY MUST ULTIMATELY FAIL

I personally believe we will see a severe decline of the U.S. economy because God's Word promises it. In Deuteronomy 28:43-45 God gave His people a warning:

> The alien who is among you shall rise above you higher and higher, but you shall go down lower and lower.
> He shall lend to you, but you shall not lend to him; he shall be the head, and you shall be the tail.
> So all these curses shall come on you and pursue you and overtake you until you are destroyed, because you would not obey the Lord your God by keeping His commandments and His statutes which He commanded you.

Observe what is happening in America. This curse is being fulfilled. Perhaps the people of this nation can turn their direction back toward the Lord. But in the long history of civilization there has never been a society that has done so.

This does not mean that there won't be people who will prosper during the decline of America; there will be. I pray it will be God's people because they willingly choose to follow His path. Our prosperity can be a great witness to many unsaved who will lose all they hold so dear—but only if we take a stand for God's way first. God's provision for our needs in a time of great turmoil will certainly be a witness, but only if we commit to using our surpluses to help others who are in need. In the final analysis, that is the only true motive for investing beyond our own needs: to meet the needs of others, in the name of the Lord.

2

Three Important Principles

There are approximately 12 basic principles of investing found in God's Word. During the course of this book I will discuss and amplify most of them at one time or the other. But this is not designed to be a Bible study on investing, or a theological debate on the principles of borrowing and lending. If you are interested in those topics, I would refer you to the bibliography listed in the Appendix. This particular work is designed as a "how-to" help as opposed to a "why-to."

Without question, the majority of people I have ever counseled who lost more than they made through investing violated one or more of the three basic principles taught in God's Word. Let me make it clear. Even if you follow the principles in the Bible there is no guarantee that all your investments will prosper. Since investing is more of an art than a science, losses are possible as the likes and dislikes of people change.

For instance, you may have invested in the Cord Motor Car Company, which did quite well in the twenties. However, as more modern production methods developed, Cord refused to change and the company failed. If you had Cord stock you lost your investment, even if you had followed biblical principles. Although God's Word guarantees no sure profits, the one thing that *is* guaranteed is peace and contentment. That's worth a whole lot more than money.

PRINCIPLE #1—SURETY

The term *surety* means "to take on a contingent liability." The most common example found in the Bible is cosigning for the debts of another person. For example, Proverbs 20:16 says, "Take his garment when he becomes surety for a stranger; and for foreigners, hold him in pledge."

The logic behind not signing surety is simple: When you sign for a debt without knowing how or when it might come due, you jeopardize your future. When it's the debt of another person, you absolutely don't know when it might come due. It's like the joke about the definition of a distant relative: a close relative who owes you money.

Let's assume that as an investor you know better than to cosign for the debts of another. Does that mean you have successfully avoided all surety? Not necessarily. When you sign *any* note payable and do not have an exculpatory clause you have signed surety.

The term *exculpate* means "to hold harmless." When you exculpate a loan it means that the lender agrees to clear you of all blame (literally to hold you harmless) if for any reason you fail to pay the loan off according to the terms of the contract.

But why would a lender be willing to exculpate a loan agreement? The fact is that most lenders won't anymore, but if they will it is only because there is more than enough collateral pledged against the loan to ensure that the lender is protected. Until the early eighties, most banks would exculpate a home mortgage contract if the buyer financed 75 percent of the appraised value or less. The assumption was that the property would always be worth more than the outstanding mortgage. Since the decline of the housing market in many areas, no commercial lenders that I know of are still willing to exculpate.

There are still some loans that require no personal guarantee (surety), but these are generally where a savings account or certificate of deposit is pledged as collateral. When cash accounts are pledged, the lender knows with certainty that the loan will be repaid—in full.

How important is the principle of surety? Surety is the primary reason many otherwise wealthy people go broke. If an investor with significant assets borrows to invest and pledges all the previous assets against each new loan, it is not a question of *if* he will go broke—only *when.*

One Christian investor, whom I'll call Martin, reflects the typical consequences of signing surety on investment loans. Martin came from a well-to-do family and inherited about $400,000. He used good business sense to parlay his inheritance into several million dollars. He was a committed Christian and well-known in evangelical circles for his giving and his personal testimony. Martin made his initial fortune in the oil business in Texas and Oklahoma and then took advantage of the blossoming real estate market in those areas to diversify and expand. By the mid-seventies his personal worth was estimated to be nearly $50 million and included oil wells, office buildings, and vast undeveloped real estate holdings in and around Dallas.

His personal net worth and unerring ability to spot good deals made him the darling of the commercial lenders. He regularly had bankers and S&L officers calling him with offers to lend huge sums of money for his development projects. At any given time he could call any of several bankers and arrange a million-dollar loan on the telephone.

The Arab oil embargo of the late seventies did nothing but enhance his financial position as his properties and oil-related assets skyrocketed in value. Using his asset base he borrowed several million dollars more to invest in oil and gas development, as well as entire city blocks of commercial real estate in the "oil patch."

Then, in 1981, the oil market collapsed as the OPEC nations began to cheat on their partners and export more oil than agreed upon. Prices plummeted in the oil industry; and commercial real estate in the oil patch, woefully overbuilt, stood empty.

Martin struggled under the debt load but was confident that eventually the oil market would recover and the recession in Texas and Oklahoma would end. After all, his family had ridden out the Depression years and survived; he would too.

But Martin had signed surety on every loan he acquired since the early eighties. When he borrowed, he pledged everything he had accumulated up to that point, whether he realized it or not.

Even so, he wasn't really worried. His properties were good, sound investments. The negative cash flow was well within his ability to manage until the economy turned around. At least it was as long as the bankers were willing to extend more credit on the basis of his total net worth.

Then the oil market collapse became front-page news as giant lending institutions failed because of non-performing loans. In their typical overreactive fashion known as "close the barn door after the horses have left," the government moved in and shut down many of the struggling savings and loans. They immediately declared all the outstanding loans due and payable. Within one month Martin found himself in default with no one willing to lend him another dime.

Property after property was foreclosed by the government regulators and suits were filed against Martin and his companies for recovery. By 1989 Martin owed the government (the Resolution Trust) nearly $60 million. His total asset base was down to less than $12 million by then; statistically he was bankrupt.

Then the next blow came from the IRS. With each foreclosed property came what is called "phantom income" through forgiveness of indebtedness. He owed the IRS nearly $4 million in taxes.

In 1990 Martin saw his home and cars being auctioned off by a court-appointed administrator. They allowed him and his family to retain their clothes and a few personal items of jewelry that were family heirlooms. Had Martin even excluded his home from surety it could have been sold for enough for his family to live comfortably for the rest of their lives. But he didn't. Every asset he owned was pledged against every loan he negotiated.

In a generation where surety is accepted as normal, a prudent investor would do well never to borrow if it means risking everything made up to that point. As Proverbs 17:18 says, "A man lacking in sense pledges, and becomes surety in the presence of his neighbor."

PRINCIPLE #2—RISK

If you are going to invest, even in a certificate of deposit, you will assume some risk. The general rule is: the greater the potential return, the greater the potential risk. That's why a corporate bond usually promises a higher percentage than a government bond. In order to attract investors they must offer a higher rate than the government does. Otherwise, why take the risk?

Risk, in and of itself, is not necessarily bad. After all, that's what the free market system is all about. The people who take the risks have the potential of great return, and therefore create more goods and jobs. But when the risk goes beyond common sense it is poor stewardship, and losses become the norm. Some people take risks that are so ridiculous they make no sense at all. It's like tossing a coin and having it land heads three times in a row and then betting double or nothing that it will do so forever. It won't, and you will eventually lose.

With a few exceptions, those who take excessive risks do so because they lack the knowledge and ability to evaluate the actual risk. As Proverbs 21:5 says, "The plans of the diligent lead surely to advantage, but everyone who is hasty comes surely to poverty."

Not long ago I was counseling with a couple in their late sixties who had lost their entire life savings in one of the riskiest investments possible—commodities speculation.

When this elderly gentleman shared how they had lost their savings I was honestly astounded. Over the years I have counseled with many high-income people who lost money (a lot of it) in commodities, but never a retired couple who had made their money the old-fashioned way, by hard work.

"Why," I asked, "would you take such a risk? Did a friend or relative talk you into it?"

"No," he replied in an apologetic voice, his head down. "I attended a one-day seminar on investing where the man said we could double our money in commodities. Since we didn't have quite enough to live on comfortably, I thought it would be a good way to make the money we needed."

"Didn't you object?" I asked his wife.

"I didn't know enough to object. I thought he was investing in some pigs since he said he was in pork bellies. And I thought soybeans would be a good investment too."

Unfortunately this couple learned the hard way that you cannot only lose what you have, but even more than you have sometimes. The husband had opened a margin account to buy commodities and lost not only their savings but owed nearly $5,000 to the exchange as well. Fortunately the broker was willing to absorb the loss and let them keep their home. Nevertheless, this husband was forced back into the sign-painting business at age 68.

Remember that risk is not the issue. Every investment carries some degree of risk. Just be very certain you know what the actual risk is, and decide if you're willing and able to absorb it. Remember the counsel of Proverbs 27:12, "A prudent man sees evil and hides himself, the naive proceed and pay the penalty."

PRINCIPLE #3—DIVERSIFICATION

In an ever-changing economy no one can say with certainty what will be a good investment over the next 10 years and what will be a loser. Over the long run there are basic areas of investing that do well. These include food, housing, transportation, health care, etc. But even a casual observer of economics will tell you that each of these areas has gone through some major cycles during the twentieth century. An investor who had his or her total funds in any one area would have found it difficult to survive during a major down cycle without a large cash reserve and very little debt.

Who would have believed 50 years ago that farmers today would not be able to sell their products for what it costs to grow them? And yet in the second half of the twentieth century we live in a starving world, with a surplus of food, but no one to buy it. Why? Because our American standard of living is so much higher than theirs that they cannot afford our produce.

Or who would have imagined that in a nation of 100 million drivers, who own 70 million automobiles, an investment in one of the big three car companies would go sour? But then along came the Japanese who took a large part of the market away, and the Big Three had to fight for their very survival.

In 1974 investors were begging oil and gas developers to take their money. The OPEC embargo was on; oil was in short supply, selling at $36 a barrel; and the major media networks told us the world was going to run out, remember? In the mid-eighties investors were calling the developers to see why they hadn't heard from them, except to ask for more money. Oil was selling for less than $20 a barrel again, and natural gas could not be sold at any price most of the time.

When the EPA began its terrorist attack on small oil and gas developers, threatening massive fines for even the slightest infractions of their unintelligible pollution standards, investors, facing potential fines of millions of dollars, panicked and shut down producing wells, plugging them with concrete just to satisfy the EPA.

The point is, there are no sure things; so diversification is essential to long-term stability. The world's wealthiest man,

King Solomon, once wrote, "Divide your portion to seven, or even to eight, for you do not know what misfortune may occur on the earth" (Ecclesiastes 11:2). That advice is still as sound today as it was 3,000 years ago. As my grandfather's generation used to say, "Never put all your eggs in one basket."

As you will see later, diversification means more than just splitting your money between stocks and bonds. It means investing in some assets that are "paper," such as stocks or bonds, and some that are real, such as real estate. It also means investing in assets that are not totally dependent on one country's economy: European stocks and bonds, Japanese companies, mortgage loans in the Eastern bloc nations, etc. This may all seem too complicated to someone with $1,000 to invest for future college needs, and it is. But for others, with $10,000 to invest toward retirement in 30 years, it is a necessity, and really is not very complicated if you know where to look.

3

Why Invest?

T here are scripturally sound reasons for investing, and there are unscriptural reasons for investing. If you are investing for the wrong reasons it's like having your ladder leaning against the wrong building. It won't matter how high you climb, you still end up on the wrong building.

RIGHT REASONS FOR INVESTING

From a biblical perspective, only three legitimate reasons to invest money exist:

Right Motive #1: Multiply to Give More

Take a fresh look at the Parable of the Talents Jesus told in Luke 19:12-26:

> A certain nobleman went to a distant country to receive a kingdom for himself, and then return. And he called ten of his slaves, and gave them ten minas, and said to them, "Do business with this until I come back."
>
> But his citizens hated him, and sent a delegation after him, saying, "We do not want this man to reign over us."
>
> And it came about that when he returned, after receiving the kingdom, he ordered that these slaves, to whom he had given the money, be called to him in order that he might know what business they had done.
>
> And the first appeared, saying, "Master, your mina has

made ten minas more." And he said to him, "Well done, good slave, because you have been faithful in a very little thing, be in authority over ten cities."

And the second came, saying, "Your mina, master, has made five minas." And he said to him also, "And you are to be over five cities."

And another came, saying, "Master, behold your mina, which I kept put away in a handkerchief; for I was afraid of you, because you are an exacting man; you take up what you did not lay down, and reap what you did not sow."

He said to him, "By your own words I will judge you, you worthless slave. Did you know that I am an exacting man, taking up what I did not lay down, and reaping what I did not sow? Then why did you not put the money in the bank, and having come, I would have collected it with interest?"

And he said to the bystanders, "Take the mina away from him, and give it to the one who has the ten minas."

And they said to him, "Master, he has ten minas already."

"I tell you, that to everyone who has shall more be given, but from the one who does not have, even what he does have shall be taken away."

This parable from the Lord tells us that God entrusts wealth to some of His stewards (managers) so that it will be available to Him at a later date. The management of wealth requires that it be invested or multiplied, as the parable reflects.

Right Motive #2: Meet Future Family Needs

The indication throughout God's Word is that the head of a family should provide for his own. To do this in our generation requires the sacrifice of some short-range spending to meet future needs such as education, housing, or a start in business.

Even though retirement is completely out of balance in our society (everyone seems to want to quit work), it would be very shortsighted for most people to assume they can earn as much at age 70 as they do at 50, or that they will be able to live off of Social Security. Good planning requires laying aside some of the surplus for future needs. Proverbs 6:6-8 says, "Go to the ant, O sluggard, observe her ways and be wise, which, having no chief, officer or ruler, prepares her food in the summer, and gathers her provision in the harvest."

The same can be said of education for our children. Not every young man or woman should attend college. But everyone needs some advanced training in our generation to reach his or her full potential. Wise parents lay a small amount aside each month to help their children reach their full potential.

No one can argue that basic housing is beyond the reach of most young couples today, and apparently will be so for the foreseeable future. Once you have reached your own financial goals you should be able to help your children purchase adequate housing for their families. As long as parents don't go overboard, there is little danger of spoiling children by helping them get into a home, especially if it's a two-bedroom, one-bath starter home.

Right Motive #3: Further the Gospel and Fund Special Needs
Most of us as Christians give to several organizations regularly. As the Apostle Paul said, "Now concerning the collection for the saints, as I directed the churches of Galatia, so do you also. On the first day of every week let each one of you put aside and save, as he may prosper, that no collections be made when I come" (1 Corinthians 16:1-2). Such giving is necessary to maintain and promote the Gospel. But often additional needs come up that require special funding. These include building programs, special emergency relief funds, opportunities to send Bibles into countries that had been closed (such as those in Europe's Eastern bloc), and so on. Investing wisely allows you to do this kind of giving, provided that you always keep some of the funds in cash reserves.

If the "church" is ever to break out of the borrowing habit then Christians who invest must maintain some surpluses and be willing to give to legitimate needs. Just think of the advantage of being able to fund *reasonable* building programs without debt. The interest saved could feed millions of hungry people and fund most of the training for worldwide evangelism.

One principle taught in Proverbs always comes to mind when I consider the biblical rationale behind investing for future needs: "There is precious treasure and oil in the dwelling of the wise, but a foolish man swallows it up" (Proverbs 21:20).

WRONG REASONS FOR INVESTING

I rather suspect, based on my observations of people I have counseled, that the majority of Christians who engage in speculative investing do so for the wrong reasons. If someone is trying to invest to be able to give more, his pattern of giving will reflect it long before he "strikes it rich." Giving is *not* easier as you make more; it is actually more difficult. A stingy person doesn't get more benevolent as he prospers, he gets increasingly more stingy. Charles Dickens understood this principle well when he wrote about Ebenezer Scrooge in his famous *Christmas Carol.* Only when someone's heart is attuned to God's are more resources an asset. As the Lord said in the Parable of the Rich Fool recorded in Luke 12:16-21: "This very night your soul is required of you; and now who will own what you have prepared?" (verse 20)

Wrong Motive #1: Greed
Greed simply means that a person always wants more than he needs. In our generation that is an easy motive to rationalize. After all, things might happen that would wipe out what we already have. So just a little more is always necessary.

As you will see as we progress through this book, ultimately God is our resource. If you lose sight of that truth no amount will ever be enough. Perhaps the most crucial question any Christian (or non-Christian) must ask is, "How much is enough?" For Howard Hughes, $2 billion wasn't enough. For Donald Trump, $1 billion was too little. Michael Milken's $100 million a year apparently wasn't enough.

At some point a Christian has to stop and decide why he (or she) is trying to make and store more. I would hate to die and find out that the epitaph on my tombstone read, "The Richest Fool in the Cemetery."

Not long ago I read about a professing Christian businessman who was reported to be worth $3 billion. I don't know anything about his living or giving habits, nor do I need to. What I do know is that he could probably get along quite well on $1 billion, or maybe even $100 million or so. I wrote him a letter (that he never answered) challenging him to give away the surplus above what he actually needed. Think of the testimony of a Christian committed enough to voluntarily give away $2 billion to spread the Gospel.

The unsaved of our world are not impressed by how much a Christian can make and keep. After all, few Christians can make as much money as a rock star. The one thing that normally does impress them is someone who gives away everything for what he or she believes in.

It has been my observation that those people who lose the most money typically do so because of greed. The get-rich-quick con men rely heavily on greed to blind the people to whom they sell. Greed is what motivates high-income professionals to risk money in abusive tax shelters. Most could pay their taxes and still have plenty to live on comfortably. But the desire to hang on to a little more tempts them to take excessive risks.

One doctor came in for counseling complaining that a Christian investment advisor had talked him into risking money in an opal mine in Brazil (that he subsequently lost). The opals were appraised at a highly exaggerated value (my assessment) and then donated to museums as tax write-offs.

On paper the deal looked great. The doctor invested $10,000, signed an unsecured note for another $90,000, and received a tax deduction of $100,000 the first year. He committed to lesser investments, but with the same ratios, over the next five years. Since he was in a 50-percent tax bracket at the time, he stood to gain well in excess of $100,000 over the next five or six years. The $90,000 note was to be repaid in Brazilian currency which was being devalued at the rate of nearly 20 percent a month. So in one year he could pay the note off with about 2,000 American dollars—all saved from taxes he would have paid anyway.

Unfortunately, the 1986 tax act killed all such abusive tax shelters and tagged the users with 50-percent penalties as well. One could argue that the law wasn't fair; what tax law is? But it is the law, and this doctor got stuck for all the original taxes, plus the penalty, plus interest—and to add insult to injury he lost the original $10,000 he invested. All told he repaid $140,000 for the two years he was in the deal. Had he paid the original taxes that were due he would have owed only $75,000.

My question to him was, "What is your complaint?"

He was taken back a little and replied, "Should I sue the advisor who steered me into such a bad deal?"

I believe that, according to 1 Corinthians 6:1, Christians shouldn't sue Christians. But I didn't even raise that issue, because there was a more fundamental issue at the heart of this problem. So I asked, "What was your motive in investing?"

"What do you mean?" he replied irritatedly. "I wanted to reduce my taxes."

"Why didn't you just give the money away, then?" I countered. "That would have reduced your gross income, and consequently your taxes."

He didn't answer so I offered an alternate explanation. "You invested out of an attitude of greed, because that's what a get-rich-quick attitude is. You expected to get something for nothing, and ended up with nothing for something."

He got up angrily and stormed out of my office, saying that he had come to me because I had introduced him to the investment advisor and I had a responsibility to help him get his money back. I knew that he expected me to confront the errant advisor, and although he didn't know it, I had already done so even before he came to see me. Unfortunately, rather than face the consequences of his actions, the advisor fled the country to avoid prosecution by the IRS.

It was almost three years later when the doctor called and asked if we could have lunch. At that meeting he apologized for his attitude and the fact that he had been angry at me for three years, particularly because I didn't seem all that sympathetic to his plight at the time. "I wanted you at least to accept some of the blame," he said.

"But," he added, "you were absolutely right. I acted out of greed, and was arrogant enough to think that I could outsmart the IRS. I have forgiven the advisor (who is still missing) and have committed myself to a more reasonable lifestyle" (an offshoot of repaying the IRS).

Then he added, "I have even forgiven you!"

I told him how much I appreciated that, and I had heard of a great investment in an atomic plasma car engine and wondered if he would be interested. "Just kidding," I added.

Wrong Motive #2: Slothfulness

It might seem strange to say that slothfulness is a motive for investing, but it is. Often people don't plan well during the earlier years of their lives and consequently, when faced with college expenses for their children or retirement, they panic and try to generate in five years what they should have saved over the previous 20. That's a little like counting on the lottery for the majority of your retirement funds.

A regular habit of spending less than you make (no matter what you make) and saving the difference is the proper investment plan. Hasty speculation, on the other hand, is characterized by Proverbs 20:4 which says, "The sluggard does not plow after the autumn, so he begs during the harvest and has nothing."

My favorite example of good planning is a pastor I met several years ago who worked with Village Missions. I was teaching a conference for some Village Missions pastors in California, and had been discussing the need to be good stewards of what God gives us, whether it is a little or a lot.

I knew approximately what each of the men attending the meeting made, because I had discussed their average compensation with the ministry's director. At that time a young pastor with a family made about $8,000 a year; an older pastor made as much as $10,000. At those income levels I knew I would not be talking about investment principles to most of them, so I concentrated on budgeting instead.

During one of the breaks a pastor, who appeared to be in his late sixties, came up and asked if we could meet to discuss his financial problems. I set up a time for later that day, knowing that I was probably dealing with a pastor facing retirement with virtually no savings and no Social Security available.

Instead, what he shared was an incredible story of how he had saved a sizable fortune out of his meager earnings over the previous 40 years.

He had invested his savings in small parcels of land in each community where he had ministered. By selling off pieces of the land they had accumulated, he and his wife had been able to send their four children through college, and one even through medical school. All with no debt!

He had recently sold off most of the remaining properties and his problem was what to do with the income his nearly $300,000 was generating in the bank!

I know of many people who earned 1,000 times what this man ever made as a pastor and retained nothing at his age. He was a diligent steward who handled a little well so the Lord entrusted more to him. As Matthew 25:29 says, "For to everyone who has shall more be given, and he shall have an abundance; but from the one who does not have, even what he does have shall be taken away."

Wrong Motive #3: Ego

Many people, Christians included, invest to bolster their pride and ego. Why else would someone who already has millions of dollars spend countless hours and risk everything he owns to make more?

I am reminded of the wealthy Texas oil family in which the brothers inherited a fortune so vast that it could not be calculated. The best estimate was somewhere between $4 and $7 billion—certainly a sufficient amount for several lifetimes. In the early seventies they risked a large amount in the commodities market and lost it. Then in the late seventies they risked their entire fortune in the silver market and lost everything. Why? To "corner" a world commodity. In other words, ego (my opinion). Certainly it was not a *need* for more money.

On a lesser scale I have observed individuals who were risking all that they had (and then some) because they were jealous of the success of others they knew. In a scriptural context that is ego. As Proverbs 29:23 says, "A man's pride will bring him low, but a humble spirit will obtain honor."

Wrong Motive #4: The Game of It

To some people, making money is simply a game. They have no particular attachment to the money; it's winning that's important to them. In many ways this is perhaps the most destructive of all wrong motives because it becomes an addiction just like alcohol or drugs. Everybody and everything becomes a pawn in the game: family, friends, even God.

I have known several people who professed to be Christians but were totally absorbed by the game of making money. There are some outside indicators that serve as warnings: They can never accept a loss; they will do whatever is necessary to win; they will cheat when necessary.

The worst thing about it is that usually these people refuse to see themselves as they really are and refuse to accept any responsibility for their actions. As Proverbs 28:6 says, "Better is the poor who walks in his integrity, than he who is crooked though he be rich." I also like what Proverbs 16:2 says, "All the ways of a man are clean in his own sight, but the Lord weighs the motives."

An individual I'll call Mike was one of the first people I counseled to whom making money was truly just a game. He came to my office one Monday after attending a Christian Financial Concepts seminar the previous weekend. His reason for coming was to share with me how good he was at the "game" of investing.

After reviewing some of the financial statements he had brought with him, I was impressed that indeed he had been extremely successful with his investments. He had parlayed a few thousand dollars into nearly $3 million in less than five years using a fairly simple, straightforward strategy. He bought distressed properties, particularly residential rentals, fixed them up, and sold them back to the tenants using "wrap-around" mortgages. Usually he could secure mortgages for more than his total purchase and remodeling costs. Essentially he had no money in the properties and nonrecourse loans. He cleared from $10,000 to $50,000 per sale.

What impressed me most about his strategy was that there was very little actual risk involved. I thought it was generous that he would be willing to share his knowledge with others so I asked him to join me at an upcoming conference. (I have since learned not to do this, but back then I was somewhat naive.)

At the conference he spent nearly an hour telling everyone how great and successful he was. Finally as his time was running out he shared just enough about what he was doing to attract a large group to him after leaving the platform. Right then I knew I had made a fundamental error in judgment. Mike wasn't interested in helping others. He was interested in letting others know who he was, and how successful he had been. His ego was showing through the thin Christian veneer.

Over the next several years Mike made an assortment of investments with some of the people who attended the first and only conference at which he taught. With virtually no exception they all later reported that, although the investments appeared to do well, they received no return for their share. Each time Mike would pressure them into paying him "management" fees that absorbed their profits.

Mike did not need the money. He lived well on his own investment income. The truth was that everything he did was for the game of it, and he was heard to say more than once to a disgruntled partner, "That's the golden rule: He who has the gold makes the rules."

Some signs that anyone should look for in dealing with the Mikes of this world are:

● A lot of braggadocio and self-promotion.

● Total control of everything and everyone where money is involved.

● A lack of accountability, including financial statements.

● A track record of using others, and never taking a loss themselves.

I will end this discussion on motives with one last comment: *Set your goals and pray about them before attempting to do any investing.* If you or your spouse sense that your motives are anything but biblical, it would be better to give the money away now rather than risk losing something far more important than money—your relationship with the Lord. There is a nonfinancial passage recorded in Matthew 5:29-30 that I believe fits this situation well:

> And if your right eye makes you stumble, tear it out, and throw it from you; for it is better for you that one of the parts of your body perish, than for your whole body to be thrown into hell.
>
> And if your right hand makes you stumble, cut it off, and throw it from you; for it is better for you that one of the parts of your body perish, than for your whole body to go into hell.

4

Risk and Return

Will Rogers and his friend, Wiley Post, had invested in several "opportunities" that Wiley had suggested, most of which lost money. Wiley Post was perhaps the best-known aviator of his day and was prone to risk-taking. Will Rogers was certainly the best-known political humorist of his day and had lived from hand to mouth so long in the early days of his career that he felt a strong compulsion to put something aside for his later years. He knew that a fickle public might shift its attention to another performer at any time.

The string of failures Will and Wiley experienced was nothing shy of miraculous. Rogers once told a reporter, "You couldn't pick that many losers by chance." One morning as Rogers and a reporter sat eating breakfast at a hotel in Washington, Wiley Post popped in to the restaurant, spotted Will, and came over to his table. Rogers could see that his friend had something on his mind, and asked, "What's up, Wiley?"

Post looked first at the reporter and then in a low whisper replied, "I just got a call from one of the biggest oil men in Oklahoma. He's got the best deal I ever heard of and wants us to have a part of it. He says the return on this deal will be bigger than anything he has ever done."

Will Rogers sipped his coffee for a couple of minutes and then responded, "You know, Wiley, I guess I'm more concerned with the return *of* my money, than I am the return *on* my money."

The reporter used that quip in his article, and it became one of the most commonly quoted bits of humor during the oil bust of the early thirties. The principle is still just as sound as ever: The return of your money is the highest priority. Anything beyond that is a blessing.

RATING SYSTEMS

There are a myriad of ways that investment advisors and counselors grade the risk of an investment. Almost without exception the degree of risk is rated based on the guaranteed return of the principle, not how much earnings the investment might yield. For example, most government securities—Treasury bills, savings bonds, and the like—are graded as the lowest risk of any investments. This is primarily because it is assumed that the government will always repay its debts. This may or may not be a valid assumption, given the current state of our government. But, nonetheless, ratings services have accepted the primary debts of the U.S. government as the baseline upon which all other investments are graded. This means that when the government offers its debt to the public, the interest rate it must pay to attract the funds it needs is usually the lowest of all securities.

Thus we can also equate rate with risk. The lower the risk, the lower the rate of return. The higher the risk, the higher the rate of return. Although this is not an absolute by any means, it is a good general rule to observe. So when you see an investment that promises a high rate of return you can logically assume it is because the risk is proportionately higher also.

Obviously other factors must be analyzed to determine true risk. One might argue that since a government bond carries a fixed interest rate its value can be eroded through inflation, which is true. So if the future worth of the money is brought into the equation, the concept of risk becomes more clouded.

On this basis, a good argument exists that gold is the most risk-free investment since it traditionally holds its value even in an inflationary economy. But nothing in the sales structure of gold guarantees the return of the original investment. Therefore it fails the initial test we prescribed: the return of our principal. So having come full circle on evaluating risk, and even though inflation may erode the buying power of an investment in government securities, such an investment still carries the lowest risk rating. Later, when we evaluate various investments, we will evaluate the risk of all other investments in relation to government securities.

Any rating system must also factor in the potential loss of principal and buying power through what is called "the future worth of money." In order to evaluate the future worth of an investment it is necessary to balance risk, return, and time.

For example, suppose that I arbitrarily assign a U.S. Treasury bill (T-bill) a risk factor of 1 (the least risk on a scale of 1 to 10). On the same level would be U.S. savings bonds, Treasury bonds, etc., because they are all primary obligations of the government. But do they all actually carry the same degree of risk? Not when inflation and future value are considered. A T-bill which matures in seven years may return between 8 and 9 percent in a given market, while the savings bonds would yield only 6 to 7 percent for the same period. Therefore it would not be logical to give both the same rating, even though they are both primary obligations of the federal government.

So let's add to our rating system another factor: *yield.* Assuming that our rate of return is a low of 4 percent and a high of 9 percent in government securities, we would then have the following rating:

T-bill: Risk = 1, Return = 7
Savings bond: Risk = 1, Return = 4

So you would be better off, all other factors being equal, to invest in the T-bill than in the savings bond. Why? Because you assume no higher risk and yet get a higher return.

When the time factor is added, the equation gets progressively more complicated. For instance, with no annual inflation (current or anticipated), a one-year T-bill paying 6 percent and a three-year T-note paying 7 percent would carry the same risk. But if the annual inflation rate was 5 percent, the three-year T-note must be considered a higher risk for "future value" because it cannot be adjusted during that time. The one-year T-bill could be adjusted annually for inflation through higher yields.

Rating any investment is not always simple, but I will return to this approach throughout the book when discussing specific investments. What any logical investor wants is a way to reduce risk while increasing yield. Just as obvious is the fact that it makes no sense to take on a higher risk without the potential for higher yield. Successful investing means determining what risk you must take to accomplish your long-term goals.

For example, a 35-year-old businessman making $100,000 a year who is able to save $25,000 annually toward his retirement in 30 years need not take excessive risks with his money. His total objective can be accomplished by investing in low-risk securities that offset inflation.

However, a 50-year-old man earning $40,000 a year who is able to save $10,000 annually toward retirement could not accomplish his objectives in 15 years without seeking a much higher rate of return, along with the higher risk. He would need to match the inflation rate, plus double his principal over the next 15 years. To do so would require a return on investment of approximately 20 to 25 percent a year. He won't do that in T-bills.

A widow, whom I'll call Betty, came in for counseling about her investment strategy. Betty's husband, Jim, had died the previous year and left her an estate consisting of $200,000 in insurance and about $150,000 in income properties. She also had their home, which was worth approximately $125,000, with a mortgage of $50,000.

Betty was 56 years old, did not desire to work, and would not be eligible for Social Security for another six years. At age 62 she would be eligible to draw approximately $600 a month in retirement benefits.

She needed approximately $1,400 a month to live comfortably. So her investment strategy had to be designed to provide her with that amount for six years (plus inflation), and then $800 a month for the rest of her life (estimated, statistically, to be 30 years).

A financial planner had recommended that she invest the life insurance in an annuity paying a guaranteed 7 percent a year for life. That would provide her with a monthly income of $1,166 for as long as she lived. In addition, with $600 a month rent from the income properties she would have a total long-term income of nearly $1,800, certainly enough to meet her needs.

On the surface, the plan she was considering was more than adequate. But I felt it had two essential flaws: First, the income properties were nearly 30 years old and required considerable maintenance. While her husband was alive he did the maintenance and leasing himself. But since she could not do the same, she was faced with an annual outlay of approximately $3,000 over the next 10 years to maintain and rent the properties. Thus her net income would be about $4,200 a year or $350 a month—a pretty poor return on an investment of $150,000 (about 2.8 percent).

The second flaw was that her annuity income was based on a single life plan. Thus, when she died, the annuity would stop. She would not be able to pass the principal or income to her children and grandchildren, a strong desire of hers. Also, since the annuity represented nearly 60 percent of her available assets, I felt that investing it in one company was too risky.

The plan we finally settled on was simple and less risky, while still accomplishing her objectives.

Step 1. She moved into one of the rental homes for three

years, making it her principal residence. She then sold it for $70,000, took her one-time tax exclusion for the sale of a residence, and moved back into her original home. She used $50,000 of the proceeds to pay off her home mortgage. That was the equivalent of a 10 percent return on investment—guaranteed.

Step 2. She sold the other rental unit for about $75,000, and after taxes and tithes had approximately $60,000 left over. With the $20,000 from the first sale, she had $80,000 to invest, which she put in T-bills at 7.5 percent interest for 10 years.

Step 3. The $200,000 from the insurance was split four ways and invested in a combination of an 8-percent annuity, government bonds at 8.5 percent, tax certificates at 14 percent, and a government-backed money market fund at 9 percent.

The total income from her investments was approximately $18,500 per year. Since she paid off her mortgage she also saved $7,000 a year in payments.

The net result was to improve her income, lower her risk, and remove the headache of rental houses. As you can see, it is possible to increase yield while lowering the risks by simple planning. In addition, since the majority of Betty's money is invested in timed deposits it can be adjusted for inflation periodically. Eventually all but the $50,000 in the annuity can be passed along to her heirs.

It is amazing how much risk the average investor is willing to assume. One would think that, having earned the money to invest by trading labor and time, most people would be extremely cautious about risking it. Unfortunately, that is not always so. All too often those who labored to earn their stake are looking to strike it rich, so to speak, so that they can stop their labor. As noted earlier, another reason that many people are willing to take inordinate risks is that they feel they have waited too long to get started on a plan. The need may be to educate their children, start a business, or retire. But the closer they get to an assumed goal, the greater the temptation to take risks.

I wish I could indelibly imprint on everyone's consciousness the three basic reasons that most people take excessive risks. If you will take the time to read the next few pages and to adopt the supporting Scriptures as your lifetime guides, you can save yourself (and your loved ones) a lot of money and grief.

In spite of all the admonitions in God's Word against excessive risk-taking, I still receive letters from Christians who heard the truth but still violated these basic principles and lost huge amounts of money. I suppose *huge* is a relative term. If you lose all you have, it's a huge amount.

PRINCIPLE #1:
GET RICH QUICK

Proverbs 23:4-5 says, "Do not weary yourself to gain wealth, cease from your consideration of it. When you set your eyes on it, it is gone. For wealth certainly makes itself wings, like an eagle that flies toward the heavens."

I have discussed the issue of "get rich quick" in other books, but I would feel remiss if I didn't cover it again, especially in a book dealing with investments. So for those who have read some of this before, forgive the repetition. For those who have not, please read carefully. This simple discussion can save you much grief and embarrassment.

It continually amazes me how gullible Christians are when it comes to get-rich-quick schemes. With rare exception, virtually all the nationwide get-rich-quick schemes begin inside Christian circles. The only logical conclusion I have been able to draw is that Christians tend to trust one another more than average non-Christians do and therefore are more easily influenced.

Perhaps one additional factor is the fact that we believe in the supernatural and will risk money in investments that require supernatural intervention. It's almost as if the more impossible the investment, the more Christians want to believe in it. This is particularly true where the promoters recite Bible verses to justify their claims.

In 1980, at the height of the Arab oil embargo, I was approached by a well-known Christian leader who told me he had been given a "revelation" from God about how to solve America's oil problems. Intrigued by his apparent sincerity, I agreed to hear his revelation. He and two other members of his leadership flew to Atlanta to present the most fantastic revelation of our generation, if it were true.

It seems that he had been approached by an angel one evening while he was praying and the angel revealed to him where the hidden oil deposits in America were located. This angel had pointed to a spot on a map where the largest oil reserves in the world lay untapped. Since it was in an area where no oil had ever been discovered previously and where the geology did not conform to any patterns established by the petroleum industry, I commented, "That would certainly explain why the oil companies have not located this vast, untapped treasure." They were looking in the "oil patch," and this was definitely not in that area.

When I asked why he felt there was oil in such an unlikely location, his response was, "Because God told me that is where it is." As far as he was concerned, that settled the issue once and for all.

"But how do you know your input is from God?" I asked.

He looked at me as if I were a heretic who had challenged the deity of Christ. "I was praying when God told me this," he said in a commanding tone.

The other two men with him nodded in agreement, certain that all my objections had been satisfied since he had received this revelation while praying. They suffered from a common delusion that prayer in itself has some supernatural meaning or power. Don't misunderstand me. I believe God can and does reveal Himself supernaturally through prayer. But the process of praying is not supernatural—God is.

"What do you need from me?" I asked, realizing further

argument was useless since their minds were made up that this was a vision from God.

"We need $3 million to drill a well in this spot," the pastor replied. "It will be the biggest oil find in the world and will make us independent of imported oil. If you will endorse this project we will be able to raise the development funds."

They had already raised nearly $50,000 from people in their church to do a prospectus and brochures. But raising the rest of the money had proved very difficult.

Since I had made an absolute commitment several years before never to endorse any investment products, this helped to extricate me from an uncomfortable situation. I told them the truth, "I never endorse any financial venture. God has not gifted me to give investment advice."

I also suggested that they retain the counsel of a good securities attorney since they were offering stock in several states and it appeared to me as if they had not completed the necessary registrations.

The pastor replied that their securities registration had been blocked by Satan's forces within the state governments, and they had decided to accept money from people in those states anyway. At that point I backed away from even listening to further discussion on the subject. Circumstances sometimes warrant opposing government rules, but only when those rules conflict with the ordinances of God. Such would be the case if witnessing were prohibited by law, if worship of God were restricted, or if babies were being aborted. But certainly securities registration would not fall into that category.

The three men went through with the securities sale and a limited drilling operation, raising nearly $600,000 from Christians who heard about the project. In one instance a pastor from another state told his people they would be failing God if they didn't invest in this oil venture. Several families borrowed against their homes to do so. One 80-year-old couple risked their entire savings in the project.

The hole was dry and all the funds were lost, along with

several pastors' credibility. Lawsuits flew like snowflakes as disgruntled Christians sued one another in violation of Paul's teachings in 1 Corinthians 6. The media picked up on the lawsuits because many elderly people had been duped into investing. As a result the cause of Christ was set back in the communities most affected. Ultimately the promoters of the venture—including the pastor—were prosecuted, convicted, and given prison sentences.

These weren't stupid people—neither the promoters nor the investors. Neither were they particularly greedy; although without a doubt, the promised returns influenced their decisions. They simply violated the basic rules that God's Word teaches on "get-rich-quick":

1. *Don't get involved with things you don't understand.* Proverbs 24:3-4 says, "By wisdom a house is built, and by understanding it is established; and by knowledge the rooms are filled with all precious and pleasant riches."

It would be difficult to talk a geologist into an investment like the one I just described. Why? Is it because he's smarter than the average doctor who risks his hard-earned money? No, it is because he has acquired wisdom and judgment in the area of his expertise.

2. *Don't risk money you cannot afford to lose.* Ecclesiastes 5:14 says, "When those riches were lost through a bad investment and he had fathered a son, then there was nothing to support him." Not too long ago I risked a modest amount of money in the stock of a company that had been manufacturing computer disk drives. The company had run into some bad times due to poor management and the stock had fallen from about $20 a share to $1. I had done business with the firm several years earlier when they were the leader in the industry and I felt that perhaps under new management they could recover. So I risked $500 in their stock. I didn't want to lose the money, but I knew I could afford to. I did.

Within one month, the company filed for bankruptcy and my stock was worthless. It was a high-risk venture, but it was not a get-rich-quick scheme. I knew the risk, could absorb the loss, and was willing to take a long-term gain.

The most common source of investment capital for get-rich-quick schemes is borrowed money. When investors risk borrowed money in anything, they are being foolish. When they borrow against their homes and needed savings (education, retirement, children), they are being stupid (in my opinion).

One pastor who invested in the oil exploration scheme I described earlier actually borrowed against his elderly mother's home to do so. That goes beyond ignorance into the realm of stupidity.

3. *Don't make a quick decision.* Psalm 37:7 says, "Rest in the Lord and wait patiently for Him; do not fret because of him who prospers in his way, because of the man who carries out wicked schemes." One of the prime elements of a get-rich-quick scheme is that the promoters want a quick decision. The way this is done is to make a potential investor believe that so many people want in on the deal that they're doing you a favor by giving you the opportunity first.

Usually the initial pitch is that you will get a discount or some other special consideration for getting in early. "But if you delay," the promoter warns, "the opportunity will be lost and you'll be left out."

In truth, there is an advantage in getting into most get-rich-quick schemes early on, because most of them don't survive long. So if you get in early maybe you can "sucker" enough friends in to make some money. But if you have a genuine concern for other people, you should discourage, not encourage, them to invest too.

The vast majority of get-rich-quick schemes are built on a pyramid base. This means that they require an ever-expanding supply of new investors (suckers) in order to sustain them. Usually those who join are given a monetary incentive to sell others on the scheme. If, for instance, you invest $5,000 for the right to sell synthetic oil, you can recoup your "investment" (and then some) by enticing others to do the same.

These incentives are offered under the most innocuous of terms, such as "finder's fees," "royalties," and "bonuses." The bottom line is simple: If you are dumb enough to risk your hard-earned money, you must know several people who are dumber than you are.

Even as I write, new schemes are roaring through the Christian community. Some are so implausible that at first glance it's hard to believe any thinking person would respond; but they do. I have long since realized that in the realm of get-rich-quick there are no schemes too ridiculous to believe.

Most get-rich-quick schemes get started with a novel idea and enough biblical jargon to make it sound plausible within the Christian community.

Some time back, a novel get-rich-quick program surfaced in churches around the country. The premise behind this particular scheme was based on making loans without interest: a thoroughly biblical concept taught in the Old Testament. In order to participate in the program, investors had to "contribute" 10 percent of the loan they needed. If, for instance, you needed a $50,000 loan (at no interest) you shelled out $5,000 up front—with no guarantee that you would ever get the loan.

Obviously, with no further elaboration than what I have presented, few people would be gullible enough to "invest" $5,000 with no guarantee of an eventual loan. What made this scheme work was the fact that others were receiving such loans and then telling their friends and families.

The concept is not a new one. In the early twenties a promoter named Ponzi came up with a similar idea. He took small amounts of money from a large number of investors, promising them huge returns on their investment. He offered interest rates of 10 percent a month in an era when 3 percent a year was a good return.

His "investment" worked well as long as he could attract ever-increasing numbers of investors. The concept was simple. He used a portion of the new money coming in to pay the existing investors their interest. With investors sharing testimonies of the great returns he had no lack of new investors (suckers).

The scheme continued to grow until Ponzi was recognized as one of the leading businessmen of his generation. He pitched elaborate parties, often entertaining the "nobs" of San Francisco's Nob Hill. Businessmen, politicians, entertainers, and grocers all fought for the right to give him their money. No one questioned how he was able to make such a fabulous return. After all, to question a golden goose was to risk losing it.

Eventually the scheme got so large that the interest payments required more new investors than existed, and cracks began to appear in the investment. Ponzi could no longer meet the ever-increasing payouts. For a while he solved the dilemma by promising even higher returns to those who would reinvest their earnings rather than drawing them out each month. But eventually those who wanted their money monthly grew beyond his ability to control, and he defaulted.

Panic struck as investors heard Ponzi could not deliver on the promises he had made. Mobs of investors stormed his business office demanding their money. Ponzi simply folded his tent and quietly walked away. The laws of that day relied on the principle of "let the buyer beware." Later, securities laws would be fashioned around the Ponzi principle.

Unfortunately, gullible people still abound today, just as they did in Ponzi's day. To believe that anyone can make interest-free loans to all who want them based on a 10-percent deposit is unbelievable—almost. Everyone wants to believe in something for nothing. In this case the promoters confused the issue with a lot of biblical jargon about prosperity. As a consequence, thousands of Christians lost what may ultimately amount to millions of dollars.

Most Christians, if they were honest, could relate similar instances of where they have lost money because of trusting a Bible-spouting huckster. The "investments" range from jojoba beans in the desert to gas plasma engines that will run on water. Perhaps the most common revolutionary idea is still the 100-mile-per-gallon carburetor. Every decade or so someone will drag that one out and bilk a lot of people out of their hard-earned money. I have often wondered why the car companies would spend millions to eke out another 3 miles per gallon on new cars when they have this great carburetor sitting in the back room!

PRINCIPLE #2:
WAITING TOO LONG

As I said earlier, risk is often related to time. I personally don't like books filled with graphs and charts, so I don't use them often. But one graph that is very revealing is the compound interest curve. Before explaining the chart, let's define our goal.

Let's assume an investor needs to save $200,000 to be able to retire at age 65 and have a $20,000 per year income. (We will also assume the average yield per year is 10 percent on his money at retirement.)

To read the chart is simple: Look at the time line on the bottom. This shows the number of years from when he starts investing until he retires. We will assume he has $5,000 a year to invest (or spend). The vertical line shows the rate of return he must have, depending on when he starts investing, in order to have $200,000 at retirement. So if he starts investing his $5,000 a year at age 30, he needs to earn 0.77 percent a year on his money. If he waits until 45 to start, he will need 6.7 percent per year. If he waits until 55 to start, he will need 28.7 percent per year.

The principle here is very simple: People who wait too long get panicky and then take excessive risks. One of the primary motivations behind state lotteries is this very mentality. Many people see the lottery as a way to make up for a lack of discipline in their earlier years. So the people living on Social Security or welfare try to hit the lottery and win a million

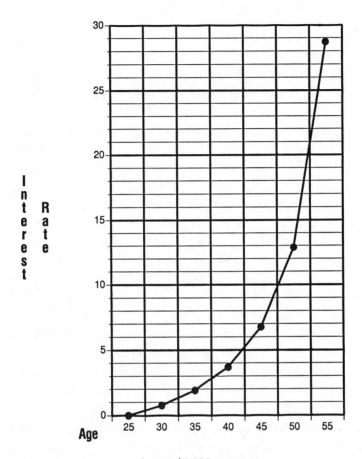

Invest $5,000 per year.

dollars (or more). The few who do are presented week in and week out as typical success stories by those promoting the system, giving false hope to those who would rather indulge now and gamble later. Obviously, what lottery promoters don't show are the millions who risk their meager earnings and lose.

PRINCIPLE #3:
EXCESSIVE RISK THROUGH IGNORANCE

Proverbs 13:15 says, "Good understanding produces favor, but the way of the treacherous is hard." As mentioned earlier, a case can be made that everyone who takes excessive risks with their money suffers from ignorance. That's probably true to some extent, but we need to differentiate between doing ignorant things (like playing lotteries or trusting in a Ponzi scheme), and being financially ignorant.

There is no dishonor in ignorance, provided you don't choose to display it. I have absolutely no knowledge of brain surgery, nor do I desire any. So I diligently avoid all suggestions that I take a Saturday off from what I do best and perform a brain operation. That obviously sounds ridiculous, but in reality that is precisely what many brain surgeons do when they risk months, or even years, of earnings in a shopping center development with no more knowledge of that specialty than I have of brain surgery.

Recently, I received a letter from an elderly couple. It seems they had retired from teaching and both elected to take their retirement savings in a lump sum, rather than take a lifetime annuity. This decision was based on the counsel of a financial planner in their church.

The annuities would have paid them a monthly income of about $600 each, which they calculated to be just barely enough to live on. Their lump sum settlement was nearly $200,000. The financial planner told them (correctly) that the lump sum could be invested safely and earn at least $1,500 a month. The additional $300 per month would mean the difference between being able to travel a little versus just paying the bills. So they took the lump sum and rolled it over into an IRA account at the savings and loan where the counselor worked. But instead of investing it in an insured account that would have been covered by the FSLIC (later the FDIC), they invested it in a bond issued by the savings and loan because it had a 2 percent higher rate of return, which amounted to nearly $300 a month more income.

Unfortunately, the S&L failed and was liquidated by the FDIC within six months of the couple's retirement. The insured accounts were covered by the FDIC, and although it took some months to get all the accounts repaid, no depositors' money was lost. But the bonds issued by the S&L were not insured since they were a debt of the corporation, not the FDIC. The corporation had no assets after liquidation and consequently this couple lost their entire savings.

They took excessive risk because of their ignorance (lack of knowledge). They could have avoided this loss simply by asking any accountant, attorney, or independent financial planner what the actual risk was.

Before you risk money in any investment, first find out what the rules are. Later in this book I'll try to provide the resources you need to evaluate any given investment area.

5

The Investment Hall of Horrors

I t's important to note that this chapter deals more with observations than it does with scientific studies. By that I mean I am offering a counselor's view of investments I have seen others make that have consistently lost money. Obviously, there are investment advisors who will disagree with my observations. That's okay too, because I would probably disagree with theirs. The criterion I use here is very simple: Of the people I have known and counseled over the years, which investments made them money and which lost?

Perhaps the simplest, most straightforward method for evaluating any investment is the percentage of people who buy into it and get their money back. The next rule of thumb is how many made a return above their investment. It's very much like evaluating your financial advisor. The rule of thumb is: If he makes you more money than he costs you, he's pretty good.

I have purposely oriented this book toward nonprofessional investors like myself. Even though I am a financial counselor and teacher, I am *not* a professional investment advisor. The difference between being a counselor and a professional investment advisor is that I don't risk other people's money.

I have always tried to limit my advice to basic financial areas such as budgets, financial goals, and biblical principles. I would personally find it rather hard to sleep at night knowing that I had the responsibility of overseeing the management of other people's money.

Most successful investors are what I call hedged risk-takers. By that I mean that they will take risks periodically if they can afford to, but they never take more risks than are considered necessary to accomplish their goals. There are investments that potentially can return great financial rewards, but most are what should be called "sucker bets." (Forgive my use of gambling terms, but that's what most of these are.)

Amateur investors who attempt to beat the odds on the high-risk investments do nothing but feed more money into the pockets of the professionals. The brokers on the commodities and stock exchanges make money whether the investors do or not. They make it when their clients buy, and then again when they sell. It matters naught whether the investors make or lose money on the transactions (as far as commissions are concerned). It would be great if a brokerage house would agree to forgo all commissions if the products they sell don't return a profit, but it doesn't work that way.

Over the years I have seen some very good investments and some very bad ones. It is impossible to categorize any single investment absolutely. Someone with specialized abilities can take a risky investment and make it less risky because of his or her knowledge and ability. As it will be throughout this book, my analysis of risk is based on the average, nonprofessional investor. If you are a thoroughly professional investor and average 25 percent a year return on your capital, you probably wasted some of it on this book. If you think you are a professional investor and average less than 25 percent a year return, you're probably fooling yourself, so read on.

THE WORST INVESTMENT: COMMODITIES SPECULATION

Commodities trading is the buying and selling of materials for future delivery. Perhaps the best book ever written on this subject for the average investor is *God in the Pits* by Mark Ritchie, a professional commodities trader in Chicago. Mark is a Christian and a good friend, and clearly one of the most successful commodities traders in America.

In chapter 1 of his book Mark describes the details of how the Hunt fortune was lost through speculative trading in the silver futures market. That one story should be frightening enough to convince any novice with less than $5 billion that commodities trading is not for the sane investor.

I have known Mark for many years, so I think I understand the mentality of what it takes to be a Christian in the commodities business. Unless you have the absolute conviction that everything you own belongs to God (literally) and can go to bed at night with the understanding that everything you have worked for most of your life can be lost while you sleep, don't trade commodities.

In the past several years, as the commodities business has become less attractive to the average investor, many speculators have shifted to trading in option contracts. An option contract gives an investor the right to purchase a futures contract at a future date. If that doesn't confuse you, nothing will.

Basically, it means that, as an investor, you pay a fee for the right to buy a contract at a future date. If the material goes up while you hold the option, you may elect to exercise the option and purchase the contract. More commonly, the option itself is resold at a profit.

The other side of options is that if prices decline you can elect to drop the option, forfeiting the option money. The advantage of options, as opposed to an actual futures contract, is that the downside risk is the amount you have paid for the option. In a futures contract the risk is potentially much greater.

Allow me to illustrate. Let's assume you purchase a futures contract to deliver soybeans in 90 days at $5 per bushel, and they are presently selling for $4 a bushel. A smart investor would buy a contract for 1,000 bushels to be delivered in 90 days at $5, and immediately purchase 1,000 bushels at market price for $4. You just made $1,000 and all you have to do is store the beans for 90 days; it's a good deal. But what if in three months soybeans are down to $3 a bushel? In that case you will have just lost $1,000.

The losses can be greatly magnified through credit. Suppose you bought the contract on margin (credit) and put down 50 percent. If soybeans go to $5 a bushel, you stand to make more than 300 percent in 90 days. If they go to $3, you can lose the same percentage! The risk is high, but so are the potential profits. If they weren't, who would be foolish enough to risk his money?

Commodities trading does have an honorable purpose, though it has been lost in the mad dash for instant riches. The commodities exchange was created to provide a method for farmers to presell their crops, thus assuring them a variable, but guaranteed, price each season. However, a quick check of the volume traded on the commodities exchange reveals that many more future delivery contracts are sold than crops are grown. What that obviously means is that many commodities contracts are never meant for delivery. They are paper transactions, designed and used only for speculation.

Trying to guess the future prices of agricultural commodities can be a stressful way to earn a living. I recall when the fighting between England and Argentina erupted over the Falkland Islands several years ago, the common logic was that soybean prices would skyrocket since Argentina was a major producer of that commodity. But, contrary to logic, after the English launched their attack the price of soybeans went down limit (the maximum allowed by the exchange in a single day's trading). Those speculators who guessed wrong, including my friend Mark, found themselves unable to sell their contracts. That's known as "catching a financial alligator." They're a lot easier to catch than to let go. Mark suffered his losses and survived, but I'm sure there were many others who lost a lifetime of earnings.

When the Gulf War broke out in January 1991 the same anomaly happened with oil. The common consensus was that oil prices would skyrocket to around $40 per barrel. Those who purchased future delivery contracts at the prevailing $26-per-barrel rate at the outbreak of the war saw prices plummet to nearly $20. That's called "wipe out."

There are ways to reduce the overall risk in commodities, such as buying options. But even so, this merely limits the downside risk. It does not reduce the risk of losing your investment money. My advice to anyone who does not own a seat on the Chicago Board of Trade is: Stay out of the commodities business. And to those who do own seats on the board—sell them and get an honest job.

WORST INVESTMENT #2:
PARTNERSHIPS

Contrary to some teachers in Christian circles, I do not believe the Bible prohibits Christians from being in partnerships. The admonition against partnerships with nonbelievers in 2 Corinthians 6:14-15 is clear, but does not extend beyond that.

Having made the point that partnerships between believers are allowable, in no way do I mean to imply that they are advisable, especially financial partnerships.

The Apostle Paul wrote to the Corinthians that "all things are lawful for me, but not all things are profitable" (1 Corinthians 6:12). That is a very good principle to bear in mind. The Lord told Peter that he should "kill and eat" (Acts 10:13). The instructions were clear that all foods and animals were allowable to eat. I would assume that would include buzzards and skunks, but they wouldn't be too palatable.

In the investment arena the most common financial partnerships are "limited partnerships," meaning that the contractual arrangement specifies a "general" or managing partner, and one or more non-managing or "limited" partners.

The intent of a limited partnership is to limit the liability of the non-managing partners to their financial investments only. Thus they would be sheltered from lawsuits, contract defaults, and future losses.

Based on observation I have often wondered if the "limited" in limited partnerships means that a participant is limited in his or her ability to get back the money invested.

Some limited partnerships require future financial participation in the event of operating losses or specified capital infusions, so they aren't all that limited. But even the limited partnerships that specify no future financial obligations have one hidden flaw—recapture.

Recapture is a nasty rule practiced by the IRS that says when a property is sold or foreclosed some or all of the previous tax deferments become due and payable, and the forfeiture of any outstanding debt becomes "phantom" income. The income may be "phantom," but the taxes aren't. They are due and payable when the loan is transferred back to the lender.

Understanding tax deferment is crucial when investing in any partnership that provides a tax write-off. There are virtually no tax eliminations where the IRS is concerned. True tax eliminations are things like tax credits, personal exemptions, operating losses, and such. All other tax reductions are called deferments, meaning that they are delayed until the investments are sold, or otherwise transferred. It's the "otherwise" that has gotten many unknowledgeable investors into trouble.

Allow me to share a typical horror story involving a limited partnership. A Christian I'll call Henry developed some limited partnerships to invest in apartment complexes. He was particularly good at taking complexes that were losing money and turning them around. The limited partners were required to invest enough money to renovate the complexes and provide enough operating capital to carry the complexes until they could be rented. There was nothing wrong with Henry's investment philosophy and, based on an estimated five-year holding period before the complexes were resold, the average return to the investors was over 50 percent a year! With that kind of return there was no lack of willing investors.

Some of the complexes were particularly desirable income properties. These were kept for income rather than sold. As the properties appreciated in value, the general partner, Henry, borrowed the original investment capital (and then some) out of the complexes and returned it to the partners. Effectively the investors had an appreciating asset that generated good income in which they had virtually no money. That's a good deal by any investment standard.

When a complex was sold the partners knew they would have capital gains taxes to pay as well as some recapture of depreciation write-offs, depending on how long the complex had been held. Since they made a sizable profit from the sale it was no difficulty to pay the taxes. But an event occurred that was ultimately to shatter the bubble of high returns with low risk.

In 1986 President Ronald Reagan proposed the most sweeping changes in the tax laws since the late sixties. One of the changes was to disallow tax write-offs from passive income investments (such as apartment complexes) against earned income. This meant that many high-income investors who bought properties and used the depreciation to shelter their regular income lost that capability. The result was an almost instant collapse of limited partnerships in general, and income property partnerships in particular. Basically there were virtually no buyers for apartment complexes that were developed to shelter taxes.

Even worse, new complexes under construction were dumped on the market at drastic discounts. Investors backed out of many new complexes and desperate mortgage lenders hired managers to rent them out at far below the going market rates. Complexes that had previously been profitable suddenly became money losers.

Many of Henry's complexes fell into arrears and were foreclosed by the lenders. Each complex that was foreclosed carried with it a tax liability for the accumulated depreciation and forgiveness of debt. The outstanding debt was considered as income to the partners when the mortgage companies reassumed the liability. The partners found themselves faced with hundreds of thousands of dollars in tax liabilities, and no money to pay them.

Many limited partners, whom I know personally, will be repaying their taxes for several years at substantial interest rates. Their homes are attached as collateral and several have had their personal assets sold at public auction. Their liability was not as limited as they had been led to believe.

WORST INVESTMENT #3:
TAX SHELTERS

Although this category includes some of the other all-time worst investments, such as the limited partnerships just described, I decided to list it separately because it is a great way to lose everything you have and then some.

Tax shelter investments are in a category by themselves simply because they are used primarily to defer income taxes rather than for any economic value they might have. It does not mean that they have no economic value. Any investment that has no economic value is prohibited, according to tax law. But if the intent is primarily the deferment of current tax liability, then I would classify that investment as a tax shelter.

Since the 1986 Tax Reform Act, tax shelters for the average investor have been much curtailed. As noted earlier, passive investment tax benefits cannot be used to shelter earned income (in most cases). Therefore, it is usually the investor with significant passive income who is attracted to existing tax shelters.

But since all things that go around come around, tax shelters for the average investor will return; of that I have no doubt. In the meantime, there are still sufficient numbers of shelters being peddled to attract the gullible.

As you might guess, I am somewhat negative about tax

shelters as investments. The reason is simple enough: I have known many fine people who have lost virtually everything they owned as a result of them. About the only people who have regularly made money from tax shelters are the salesmen, attorneys, and accountants.

Tax shelter investments prey on the uninformed and the greedy (my opinion). The simple truth is that unless you are willing to spend years in court and lots of money on accountants and attorneys, you will not beat the IRS at their own game for two basic reasons. One, they can use your own money to fight you. Two, they have the ability to change the rules in the middle of the game.

I can think of a hundred personal examples of people I have known who thought they could "beat the system." But in the interest of time and space I will share only one.

A Christian professional athlete whom I'll call Bob was being counseled by a "Christian" investment advisor on how best to maximize his income during his professional career. Bob was a fairly typical pro football player—though intelligent and skilled at his sport, he had practically no business experience. His salary of nearly $200,000 a year seemed enormous when compared to the pittance he and his wife had been living on in college. But after paying his taxes, tithes, normal living expenses, and additional in-season living expenses, he had less than $10,000 a year left over to invest.

Unfortunately for Bob, his investment advisor followed a strategy of using multiple tax shelters to save as much tax as possible and then using the tax money to invest for the future.

He put Bob into a Brazilian opal mine that would shelter $10 in taxes for every $1 invested (using leveraged notes payable). Next he suggested Treasury bill straddles (if you don't know what these are you're better off). These provided an artificial loss at the end of each tax year. Finally, he put Bob into a highly leveraged equipment leasing deal that would shelter nearly $20 in taxes for every $1 invested (again using future debt and investment tax credits).

The result was that Bob saved all of his tax liability (federal and state). This provided him with an additional $70,000 a year to invest (less the $30,000 it took to invest in the tax shelters). Bob was convinced that his advisor was a wizard.

The advisor then helped Bob invest in several real estate and business deals for which the advisor received a commission. He also had received either commissions or finder's fees for placing Bob in the tax shelters. I always thought it interesting that during this time the advisor did not invest in any of these tax shelters himself, although he did risk some money in the more traditional investments.

Bob retired from professional football in 1984, expecting to be able to live off of his investments and whatever income he could earn as a teacher and coach. Instead he got the biggest shock of his life: a letter from the IRS stating that he was being audited.

The audit quickly progressed from bad to nasty, with the agent recommending that the IRS disallow all of the tax shelters. He further recommended that 50-percent penalties be assessed, along with interest.

Bob quickly hired a tax attorney to represent him before the IRS. After investigating the shelters the attorney recommended that Bob plead for mercy. It seems that in the case of the T-bill straddles the investment company hadn't even bothered to make the trades each year. They just sent a falsified report to Bob's accountant. Even if they had made the trades the IRS would have disallowed the deduction as a sham transaction, but in this case there was no defense—not even ignorance.

When the dust settled Bob owed more than $200,000 in taxes, interest, and penalties, with the interest clock continuing to tick.

Unfortunately, Bob's money was gone by then. He couldn't get his investment money back, and the tax shelter companies had folded and fled into the night. Bob lost his home, cars, investments, and even had his retirement account with the

NFL attached for taxes. He now works a full-time job, with the IRS receiving nearly one fourth of his total take-home pay.

WORST INVESTMENT #4:
PRECIOUS METALS

I know I'm going to irritate some friends who believe in precious metals as investments. But I have to say what I believe, and thus far most of the people I know who have made money on precious metals are those who sell them.

There are two basic reasons why people invest in precious metals such as gold and silver. The first, as with any other commodity, is to speculate on their rise and fall. The second is as a hedge against a future collapse of the economy and/or the currency system.

One negative aspect of speculating in precious metals is the cost of buying and selling them. Unlike stocks and bonds, which have a well-organized and highly competitive market, precious metals have no such market. Investors can buy contracts for future delivery of precious metals in the commodities exchange, just as for virtually any commodity, but buying the actual metal is limited to a relatively few traders around the country.

These traders or dealers mark up the metals, usually from 5 to as much as 12 percent, when they sell them. Then when they repurchase the metals they make an additional premium by way of a discount from the quoted retail price. Essentially investors buy at retail and resell at wholesale. It takes a significant rise in price to make up the fees.

I know there are individual exceptions to this rule, but discount brokers and buyers are not available to the average precious metal investor.

In the case where an investor is buying precious metals as a hedge against a potential economic disaster, there is some justification for not listing them among the "worst" investments. After all, we haven't had a real depression since the thirties, so we don't know how metals will fare. So in fairness to those who sell gold and silver as a hedge against a collapse, I will downgrade my evaluation to merely a "questionable" investment.

Those who bought gold at $30 an ounce and saw it climb to over $500 an ounce in the seventies would probably disagree. But again, for the average investor who bought in after that one spectacular event, the trend has been level—to down.

Even the most enthusiastic precious metals advocates rarely defend the purchase of silver anymore. So many novice investors got wiped out in the great fall of silver in the early eighties that most dealers speak of silver in whispers only. In reality the depressed price of silver probably makes it one of the better speculative risks for the next decade.

The difficulty with buying precious metals (primarily gold) as a hedge against collapse is one of determining the future of gold as a currency. Traditional hard money advocates say that when a nation's (or world's) currency gets too inflated it will collapse and people will return to the gold standard. Unfortunately, that theory was developed before the communications age that we are in today. It is my strongly held conviction that the next currency will be neither gold nor paper. It will be electronic transfers, regulated and controlled by a central world bank.

If that proves to be true, and only time will tell, gold will be little more than a speculative commodity again. Those who don't believe this could happen need to read the arguments from the thirties that the United States could not remove its currency from the gold standard. We did it because of the desire to put out massive amounts of paper money without the requirement to collateralize it with gold. The same mentality (political necessity) may well divorce all world currencies from the confinements of a limited supply of gold. I am not advocating this reasoning. I am simply looking at the facts and stating my opinion.

WORST INVESTMENT #5:
GEMSTONES

A woman may well treasure the diamond she wears on her finger or around her neck, but it is *not* an investment. For the average investor the same can be said of most precious and semiprecious gemstones. Most novice gem speculators usually buy high and sell low.

There are several factors that encourage me to list gems in my worst investment category, not the least of which is the difficulty for the average investor to tell the quality and value of gems.

There are grading organizations that will swear to a gem's quality, clarity, and estimated value. But unless you can resell to the same dealer that sold the stone to you, the next trader may not accept the evaluation. Even if the original dealer does agree to repurchase the gem(s), there is no guarantee that he will give you the current market value. The market value of gems is nebulous at best, and is not quoted daily as are company stocks.

In the mid-seventies several large traders, pooling their resources, made an attempt to create a ready market for precious gems—particularly diamonds. Unfortunately, all that came of it was a dramatic increase in the price of diamonds as the companies marketed them aggressively. Many individuals bought "investment grade" diamonds after being assured they were secure investments. "After all," the salesmen said, "diamonds have held their value better than any other investment over the last 100 years." This was true to a large extent because the DeBeers trading company of South Africa controlled the supply of diamonds very carefully, allowing only a few investment-quality stones on the market each year.

The net result of this debacle can best be demonstrated by a gift a supporter made to our ministry a few years back. He bought a one-carat "investment" quality diamond in 1982 for approximately $16,000. It was sealed in a plastic container along with a certificate issued by a certified appraiser.

In 1986 he donated the diamond to our ministry. We attempted to sell it at what was estimated to be its fair market value of nearly $20,000 (based on the opinion of the original dealer). Two prospective buyers sent the stone to be reappraised. The first appraisal downgraded the stone's quality one full point, lowering the value to about $9,000. The second came back two points down, with a value of $5,000. There were no buyers at either price, I might add.

I told the shocked donor, who immediately went to the dealer who sold him the stone. He had a written option to resell the diamond to the dealer at the original sales price at any time. The dealer told him a sad tale about his misfortune with other investors and notified him that he had filed for bankruptcy.

Over the last 20 years or so I have counseled many people who have purchased gems as investments. Some were happy because the gems were safely locked away in their safety deposit vaults appreciating greatly, according to the reports they received annually from their dealer/broker. And I am quite sure that many investors who resell their gems to friends and family do make a profit. But to date I have not met a single novice (nonprofessional) investor who has made money on gems, except by reselling to another friend who didn't know better either.

WORST INVESTMENT #6:
COINS

Collectible coins, stamps, and other unique items can be good investments for knowledgeable buyers who take the time and effort to become proficient at their trade. It is not to this group that I speak. Nor is it to those who collect coins and stamps for a hobby. Basically they don't care if the items appreciate or not. Obviously anyone would rather their assets appreciate, but if they are not going to sell them, who cares?

I restore old cars as a hobby, and I really don't intend to sell them. I periodically check to see what equivalent cars are selling for, but only by way of interest. Most of the cars have so much of my labor in them that at double the market price I would net about a dollar an hour for my time. For me, it's a hobby, not an investment.

There are several companies that offer numismatic (collectible) coins as investments. In the eighties collectible coins became very popular investments not only because they could appreciate in value as collectibles, but also because the coins usually contained precious metals.

There is no doubt that many numismatic coins have appreciated over the last two decades, so why list them among the worst investments? Because, in general, it is the professional collector who has done well, not the novice investor. In recent years many trade shows have developed to buy and sell coins. These establish a market for coins and have helped to standardize the pricing through a very detailed grading system between traders.

But if the market for collectible coins were limited to dealers only, the prices would quickly settle down with little or no appreciation. Why? Because the traders would all know the true value of the coins and would not sell too low or buy too high (except for extreme cases of hardship).

For the price spiral to continue, it is necessary to market the coins to the general public. Thus a trader buys coins at their true market value at a show, then resells them to investors (usually through a recruited mailing list) at higher prices. If enough investors can be found, the dealer makes his own market.

If a novice investor attempts to resell a coin at the listed market price, he quickly discovers that what he paid was retail and the price he is offered is wholesale. The dealer buys low and sells high, so the investor is forced to resell to the dealer at a substantial discount.

If the dealer would give his investors access to his mailing list, they might be able to command his prices, but he obviously won't. Some dealers *will* offer to resell your coins, or even repurchase them at the wholesale price. But unless the coins have appreciated greatly, you end up either losing some of your investment or, at best, making a small gain.

Again, drawing on the testimonies of many people I have counseled who purchased coins for investment purposes, the vast majority said they lost money; some of them, a lot of money!

If you're not interested in studying numismatic coins, you'll probably find they are not a good investment for you. One side note is necessary here. If you ask a friend who bought coins, he will probably tell you he did well. That's because compared to some of the other investments he made, the coins lost the least. That is not exactly what you're looking for from your investments.

WORST INVESTMENT #7:
STOCKS

Since I have already alienated a large part of my friends who sell investments, I figure that I might as well go the whole way and irritate the rest—so I have included stocks among my worst investments list.

Again, I would emphasize that a knowledgeable, professional investor can and does make money regularly on common stocks. Also, anyone can learn how to evaluate stocks and reduce the risks involved. But for the average investor, today's market is not like that of our fathers' day. Determining which stocks will do well and which will not is a highly technical field that very few investors are equipped to handle.

I would also like to make it clear that I am *not* trying to discourage those who invest in a single stock, such as that offered by the company they work for. I am referring to novice investors who buy stocks based on their "gut" feelings. More often than not, what they are feeling are simple gas pains.

If you took a portion of your savings and bought a representative sample of "blue chip" stocks and then just held on to them for 20 years you would do fairly well. From 1970 to 1990 your investment would have kept pace with inflation and earned about 3 percent a year in real growth. Unfortunately, the average investor doesn't do that. He hears of a strong bull market and jumps in, trying to make a big hit. Usually by the time he hears about the bull market it has peaked, so he gets in at the top. Then the market turns down and he sells in a panic to avoid taking the big loss. It has been my observation that the net transaction is a loss, with rare exception.

If you are one of those people who can dollar average your stock purchases, meaning that you continue to invest in the blue chips during good times and bad, you will do okay. But it also means that you have probably just moved out of the average or novice category, in which case you would be better off switching your investment over to mutual funds where a knowledgeable professional with a proven track record will manage your stocks for you.

You may or may not agree with my worst investment list, but I developed it by observing how others have consistently lost their hard-earned money over the years. Some people have beat the system and walked away with their earnings. But on the average the people I counsel are not professional investors, and they range in incomes all the way from half a million dollars a year to less than $10,000. Some are college graduates, some have not completed high school. Some are senior citizens, others are just starting out. The point is they represent the average American investor pretty well, both Christian and non-Christian. Most would heartily agree that had they avoided these "worst investments" they would have been much better off financially today. But that decision is up to you. As Proverbs 18:15 says: "The mind of the prudent acquires knowledge, and the ear of the wise seeks knowledge."

6

The Best Investments

Since I don't want to seem anti-investment oriented, I decided to include a chapter on those investments that have worked out best for those I have counseled. This in no way implies that everyone who selected one of these investments made money with it, any more than those who selected the previous group always lost money. But on the average, more people made money using these investments than lost money.

THE BEST INVESTMENT:
A HOME

Without question the best overall investment for the majority of Americans has been their home. Residential housing has kept track with inflation and appreciated approximately 4 percent a year besides. That doesn't make it the best growth investment, but it does make it the best performer for the average individual.

It is also important to remember that our homes serve a purpose beyond the investment sphere. A home is something that you can use while it appreciates.

Many investment analysts have recently commented that the boom in residential housing is over. That is probably true to some extent. I believe that the expansion of single-family residences via cheap credit is winding down and housing will be more expensive for young couples. But Americans are hooked on having their own homes. If that trend changes it will only be because the country is in the midst of another Great Depression, in which case all other investments are equally at risk.

It is unfortunate that most Americans have been duped into accepting long-term debt on their homes as normal. With the prices of homes being what they are today, most young couples need extended loans to lower their monthly payments initially. But any couple can pay their home off in 10 to 15 years simply by controlling their lifestyles and prepaying their principal a little bit each month.

A simple investment strategy to follow is to make the ownership of your home your *first* investment priority. Then use the monthly mortgage payments you were making to start your savings for education or retirement. If you can retire your home mortgage before your kids go to college, they can graduate debt-free (and you too).

The most common argument against paying off a home mortgage early is the loss of the tax deduction for the interest. Allow me to expose this myth once and for all.

Let's assume that you are in a 30-percent federal tax bracket and a 6-percent state tax bracket. We'll also forget that the tax rates are graduated (based on a lower percentage at lower incomes). For each $1,000 in interest you pay on a home mortgage you will receive 30 percent of it from the IRS and 6 percent from the state, right? ($1,000 x 30% = $300; $1,000 x 6% = $60) So you will net $360 for your $1,000 interest payment. What happened to the other $640 you paid in interest?

As best I can tell, the mortgage company kept your money and you only received a portion of it back through tax deductions. What would happen if instead of paying interest on a mortgage you simply paid the taxes?

You would owe $360 in federal and state income taxes, but

would keep $640. I'm not an investment counselor, but that seems like a better deal to me.

Retiring your home mortgage early pays huge investment dividends. Suppose, for instance, that you have a 30-year mortgage at 10 percent on a loan of $100,000.

The first of the following two illustrations shows how much a 35-year-old man retiring at age 65 could save in a retirement account at 6 percent if the home mortgage was retired early by paying an additional $100 per month and then the mortgage payments he had been making were saved in the retirement account.

- $100,000 mortgage at 10% for 30 years = $315,720
- $100 per month additional payment saves $90,033 in interest. Home is paid off in 19 years.
- Mortgage payment of $877/month + $100/month prepayment invested in retirement account at 6% for 11 years = $182,947 (approx.)

NET RESULT: Home paid off (at age 54, at total cost of $225,687) and $182,947 in savings by age 65.

The next illustration shows the comparison if, instead of prepaying the mortgage, the same person continued to pay the mortgage for 30 years while putting the $100 extra in a retirement account.

- $100,000 mortgage at 10% for 30 years = $315,720
- $100 per month invested in retirement account at 6% for 30 years = $100,953 (approx.)

NET RESULT: Home paid off (at age 65, at total cost of $315,720) and $100,953 in savings by age 65.

CONCLUSION: Paying off the mortgage *before* saving for retirement nets an additional $81,994 toward retirement (*plus* the savings on the mortgage).

The bottom line is, you're a lot better off financially earning interest than you are paying it. As Proverbs 9:9 says, "Give instruction to a wise man, and he will be still wiser, teach a righteous man, and he will increase his learning."

BEST INVESTMENT #2:
RENTAL PROPERTIES

It has often been said that the thing you know best, you do best. The majority of Americans know how to evaluate rental properties, particularly residential housing. Most of us have been renters ourselves at one time or another, or have bought and sold homes. Most homeowners have the ability to evaluate good rental real estate; at least when compared to buying soybeans, stocks, or coins. Therefore, rental properties are a logical source of investments—but not for everyone.

There are assets and liabilities to owning rental properties. Unless you have a strong personality and are willing to eject some nonpaying tenants from time to time, you need to avoid becoming a landlord.

A friend who has done exceedingly well in residential rentals over the years has a philosophy that I endorse. First, he sets his rent levels at less than the going market rates in his area. This is so he will attract a good volume of potential renters and can then qualify them according to the criteria he has established over the years, which include credit checks, previous rentals, and personal references. His low-rent policy also helps to attract long-term tenants who know they could never duplicate the deal he has provided them.

He establishes his rental rates on the basis of covering his mortgage payments and other out-of-pocket costs, including that of maintaining the properties. His goal has always been to use the rental income to pay off the mortgages, and then use the mortgage payment money for his retirement income. During the first 10 to 15 years he receives very little, if any, personal income from the rentals. Yet he now owns several dozen rental houses debt-free and has a sizable, and very stable, income.

Often he has shared stories of renters who have maintained the properties at their own expense, including one who totally reroofed a home because he did not want his rent to go up. This is one of the rare win-win situations with rental properties.

One of the most attractive aspects of rental property is that the initial investment is not excessively large in many areas. An additional benefit is that once the property is rented the tenants pay off the mortgage for you.

Many investors have moved up from single-family rentals to duplexes or triplexes because the risk is reduced. The chances of a unit being vacant are cut proportionately to the number of tenants it will accommodate. The flipside of the coin is that the initial costs also go up, and often to buy such a unit requires a partnership arrangement with someone else.

One additional idea is to joint venture a rental home with a couple who will live in it. Usually this means the investor provides the down payment and assumes a 50-percent (negotiable) interest in the property. The tenant couple then pays the mortgage payments and all other associated costs, including maintenance. When the house is resold, usually after no more than 10 years, the investor receives the down payment back and the two parties split the profits equally. There is a risk that the property will not appreciate, but that is the risk you run with any investment.

BEST INVESTMENT #3:
MUTUAL FUNDS

The whole concept of mutual funds is designed to attract the average investor. The pooling of a large number of small investors' moneys to buy a broad diversity of stocks (and other securities) is a simple way of spreading the risks.

Most of the average-income families I know who have accumulated supplemental income for education or retirement have done so successfully through the use of mutual funds. I particularly like mutual funds because (1) most allow small incremental investments, (2) they provide professional investment management, and (3) they allow great flexibility through the shifting of funds between a variety of investment assets.

As with any other area of investing, you must exercise caution and acquire some fundamental knowledge of what you're doing. There are funds that perform well in good economies and then lose it all in economic downturns. There are funds that guessed right once and basically never duplicated the feat again. There are funds that charge excessive administrative fees and dilute the return to their investors. And there are funds that have performed well for two and three decades and continue to lead the industry.

Even with these, you must exercise some caution, because their success may be built around the expertise of a single individual. When that person retires or dies, the fund may lose its edge. It is well worth an investment of $50 to $100 a year to subscribe to a good mutual fund newsletter if you have $10,000 or more to invest. It will help you to keep close tabs on the fund(s) you select. A list of some suggested newsletters is included in the Appendix.

Mutual funds offer such a diversity of investment products that it is probably safe to say that if you want to invest in anything legitimate there is a fund that will allow you to do so. Since we're going to evaluate some of the various fund types that are available in a later section, I will not elaborate here.

It is important to note, however, that in placing mutual funds in the best investments category I need to offer a qualifier. A good-quality, well-managed fund fits in that description. A poor-quality, poorly managed one does not. Later we will discuss how to find the funds that have proven to be the most reliable to the average investor.

Just remember that just as stocks are more speculative than corporate bonds, and bonds are more speculative than CDs, and CDs are more speculative than Treasury bills, mutual funds fit the same profile. So the type of fund you invest in will greatly affect the risk of your money, even in the well-managed ones. The higher the promised return, the greater the risk that must be assumed.

A growth (speculative stock) mutual fund managed by the best advisor in the world is still more risky than a mutual fund that invests only in U.S. Treasury securities. When we get into the strategy planning section of this book it is important to keep this in mind.

The question of whether to invest in a loaded or no-load fund always comes up in any discussion of mutual funds. A "loaded" mutual fund means that the sales commissions and administrative fees are taken out of the purchase price of the fund up front. For instance, a $5,000 investment in a fund with a 6-percent load would actually leave $4,700 to be invested in the fund. Additionally, you may also be charged an annual fee that can vary from a few dollars to several hundred or more, depending on the amount invested.

A "no-load" fund means that no commissions or fees are deducted up front. Logically an investor should therefore conclude a no-load fund is better since 100 percent of your money goes into the investment. That may or may not be true in the long run. If the no-load fund has higher annual fees and commissions, the money you save up front can quickly be consumed in the first few years, and then some.

I have personally found that a well-managed no-load fund will beat a well-managed loaded fund; therefore, that is what I look for. But a well-managed loaded fund is a better buy than a poorly managed no-load. So choose your fund carefully. The primary reason a loaded fund is loaded is because of salesmen's commissions. If you need individualized help in selecting or understanding mutual funds, the fees may be worth it to you. The no-load funds sell their products through advertising, not agents. They will provide any information you need by phone or mail, but use no local sales agents. It is my opinion that a subscription to a good mutual fund newsletter is better than paying a commission, but you may disagree if you know an honest, knowledgeable agent.

As with most investments today, one of the primary difficulties with mutual funds is trying to decide which type of fund best suits your individual need, and then which company's products are the best. With the hundreds of choices and every salesman (by phone or in person) totally convinced that his or her products are the best, it can be very confusing. Using the resources listed in the Appendix can help you sort it out.

BEST INVESTMENT #4: INSURANCE PRODUCTS

I have found in teaching a daily radio program on finances that there is no better way to stir up a heated debate than to discuss insurance. It really doesn't matter what position I take: If I am for insurance or against it (or totally neutral), I'm always stepping on somebody's toes because so many people earn their livings in the insurance industry.

If you would care to read a thorough discussion on insurance from a biblical perspective, as well as the assets and liabilities of term versus whole life, see my book, *The Complete Financial Guide for Young Couples* (Victor Books, 1989). But for the purposes of this particular book I'll limit my evaluation to the investment side of insurance.

Over the past 20 years or so, insurance companies have developed many investment products to tap into the private retirement savings movement. Products like cash-value insurance and annuities have been around for nearly a hundred years, but they were not really competitive as investment vehicles until more recently, in my opinion.

Generally speaking, the accumulated savings in life insurance was, and still is, too accessible to the investor. Therefore, the majority of investors look upon their cash values as a ready source of funds in a time of need. That's fine if the intent is to build a reserve account for a new car, a down payment for a home, or even a college tuition fund. But there are many places to save money at higher rates of interest than a whole life insurance policy. Besides, stripping life insurance of its cash values reduces the amount of insurance available in the event of the insured's death.

During the decade of the eighties, as retirement plans such as IRAs, Keoghs, 401Ks, and the like became available to the general public, the insurance companies realized they had to pay higher rates of return if they were to be competitive as investment companies. The insurance companies also realized that the higher yielding mutual funds would eventually pull capital out of existing insurance policies. A knowledgeable investor would not leave money in a cash-value insurance policy at 4 to 6 percent return when mutual funds were earning twice that per year. Consequently, the major insurance companies began to offer policies with much higher yields. With the dual benefit of insurance coverage, plus higher yields, they became viable products for long-term investors.

The two basic types of insurance plans used most often (by those whom I have counseled) are annuities and whole-life insurance (usually in specialized policies such as universal life). There are endless varieties of these plans available. The difficulties are to determine which best suits your investment needs, and then to decide which company offers the highest return with the lowest risk. I have included a section on evaluating investments, which covers insurance products, so I will not elaborate on them here. Generally speaking, insurance products have been among the safest, if not the highest earning, investments. But what has been safe in the past does not automatically imply future safety. The insurance industry as a whole is very sound, but several of the larger companies have made many bad investments. The future of some insurance companies is in jeopardy. It is critical to select the company you use carefully and continue to monitor it at least annually, just as you would any other investment.

It would be far better to withdraw your cash reserves from a policy, or transfer your savings in an annuity, even if there is a penalty to do so, than to risk losing it all. The Appendix provides all the sources necessary to evaluate your insurance company, should you choose to use these types of products.

BEST INVESTMENT #5:
COMPANY RETIREMENT PLANS

It almost seems unnecessary to list company-sponsored retirement plans among the best investments, but it continually amazes me how many people don't take advantage of the opportunities to use them. The jargon used to identify these plans may be confusing, with titles like 401K, 403B, TSA, HR-10, and the like. But, in reality, the titles simply reference the tax codes that authorize the plans.

The investments available through a company retirement plan are the same as those you might choose personally. Depending on the plan and how it is administered, your options can include annuities, mutual funds, company stock, CDs, or any combination of these.

The disadvantage of a company retirement plan is that although you may be able to select any of several investment options, the plan administrator(s) select the plan's options. They may or may not be the best options available to meet your personal goals.

One large advantage of company-sponsored retirement plans is that usually the funds invested are tax deferred (delayed until withdrawal). Additionally, many companies offer matching funds based on a percentage of what you elect to invest yourself. Some companies even go so far as to provide 100 percent of the retirement funds. I trust there is no one foolish enough to turn down an offer like that.

There are some potential problems with company retirement accounts. You need to be aware of these and take the proper precautions.

1. *The plan administrator may invest poorly, thus placing your funds in risk.*

2. *The company may reserve the right to borrow from the employees' retirement account for operating capital.* The problem here is that if the company fails, the retirement plan may fail too, especially if the company has substituted its own stock as collateral for the loans.

3. *The company may reserve the right to borrow from the retirement account and substitute an insurance annuity for the cash.* If the insurance company itself fails, then the retirement plan fails too.

Even with these potential problems, company-sponsored retirement plans represent one of the best investments for any average investor. Most companies are run honestly and ethically and have the best interests of their employees at heart. Just be aware of the potential problems and do the checking necessary to verify the solvency of your plan.

Remember, the sooner you start in a retirement plan, the less risk you will have to assume in order to reach your financial goals. Sometimes it is advantageous to invest in a company retirement plan even before paying off a home mortgage, especially if the company matches the funds at a rate of 25 percent or more. It's hard to beat an investment where someone guarantees you a 25-percent return the first year—tax-free!

BEST INVESTMENT #6:
GOVERNMENT-BACKED SECURITIES

In pondering what to include in the best investments section I have tried not to get too detailed, lest we both get bogged down in whether a municipal bond from Chicago is better than one from New York. That kind of analysis is difficult at best since risk factors can change so quickly. So I purposely limited the discussion to general areas of investment. As I said earlier, government-backed investments are considered to be absolute security. Among those I have counseled who were older than 50 years of age, government-backed securities dominated their best investments list.

This does not imply that securities such as CDs, T-bills, bonds, and the like are the best performers. As mentioned earlier, they are usually selected for their lack of risk, not their return.

Once you have saved enough to meet your investment goals, whether they be college education for your children, retirement, or otherwise, the shift to government-backed securities is logical. Why leave your money at risk if you don't need to? Obviously your plans need to compensate for inflation, but the ratios should swing decidedly toward the safe side as you get older. Simply put, it is more difficult, if not impossible, for most older people to replace their investment funds; so the older you are, the more conservative you should become in your investing.

7

Strategy
for Investing

It has been my observation that anyone who hopes to accomplish any goals, short-term or long, must have a strategy. The strategy may be as simple as that of a counselee I once met, who said, "I'm going to spend what I make and count on the Lord's return before I'm 65." That strategy may or may not work; we'll have to wait and see. But since it depends on events over which we have no control, I don't advise it for most people.

The principle taught in Proverbs 6:6-8 is one more suited to most of our needs: "Go to the ant, O sluggard, observe her ways and be wise, which, having no chief, officer or ruler, prepares her food in the summer, and gathers her provision in the harvest." Since we *don't* know when the Lord will return, and we *do* have specific needs later in life, we are instructed to save some of what we make in our harvest years for use later. Many Christians mistakenly believe that accumulating a surplus is somehow "unspiritual." It may be, if the attitude is one of hoarding. Hoarding means that the *goal* is to create a surplus. In contrast, saving is anticipating a future financial need and preparing for it.

Before discussing strategies for investing, I would like to discuss some biblical justifications for investing. I was once challenged by a dedicated Christian who was convinced that storing assets for the future was contrary to God's will. He said God expects us to take any and all surpluses and put them into His work immediately.

Somehow I knew this was incorrect, but he was a more mature Christian than I was and I respected his opinion, so I decided to do a study on the subject. I found that there is no biblical basis for his statement.

While it is true that God's Word teaches we should share with those in need, and give graciously to do God's work, it also teaches that we are to look ahead, identify future needs, and plan for them. The key is to identify *needs*—not greeds.

The Parable of the Rich Fool in Luke 12:16-21 tells us that once we have "enough" we should not store more. To do so *is* hoarding. But the Parable of the Prodigal Son in Luke 15:11-24 tells of a father who obviously had a surplus that he was storing for his sons. There is no hint of condemnation toward the father in this parable, just as there is no implied condemnation in the previous parable of the farmer's wealth. A survey of God's Word shows clearly that often God promises wealth to those who serve Him. Solomon asked for wisdom instead of riches, so God granted him both. Job was rewarded for his faithfulness with twice his original wealth. Jacob was made to prosper in Laban's employment. The examples go on and on.

If you need further evidence that God does not condemn reasonable saving for the future, consider Abraham, David, and even Barnabas in Acts 4:36-37. It would be very difficult to do God's work without some storage for future needs.

I particularly like the balance taught in Proverbs 11:25: "The generous man will be prosperous, and he who waters will himself be watered"; and in Proverbs 21:20: "There is precious treasure and oil in the dwelling of the wise, but a foolish man swallows it up." So it isn't the surplus that creates the problems. It is the attitude!

It is a sad commentary on self-discipline in America that the average American is worth less at age 65 than he was at 25. The dependence on government programs and acceptance of indulgent lifestyles have deceived most Americans into believing that someone else will take care of them. If God has provided for our future needs by providing a surplus during our harvest years, we shouldn't expect Him to come and bail us out because we wasted it.

There are many who cannot provide totally for the future because they have very little during their working years. But everyone can save something! What they lack later God will provide—if they were faithful with the little they had earlier. Often God will use those who were blessed with large surpluses to help those who have virtually none.

I recall a missionary I met in 1974 who had spent nearly 40 years in Central America, often living on less than $1,000 a year. At age 62, because of health problems and ministry policy, he and his wife returned to the States. He was facing retirement in a highly inflated economy on an annuity of $120 a month. That may have been adequate in 1934 when he began his work, but it would barely pay his utilities 40 years later.

He and his wife had been good stewards of what they had. They just never had much money. The question I asked him was, "If you had the chance to relive your life knowing what you now know, would you return to the mission field?"

He immediately replied, "Absolutely. I believe I was doing what God called me to do."

"Then," I said, "God has the answer. He will not abandon you now."

By 1977 he had turned a hobby, collecting ceramic figurines, into an income of more than $200,000 a year. God had known of his need and had made plans to meet it. But the key was that he had been faithful with the small portion first.

BIBLICAL REASONS
FOR INVESTING

Motive #1: Giving
I discussed this principle earlier, but I would like to explore it further because it forms the foundation of any strategy. In

truth, most of the giving in America is not done by those with the greatest surpluses. In a survey conducted for the National Family Council in 1989, it was shown that those with incomes above $100,000 annually gave about 2 percent of their incomes. Those with incomes between $10,000 and $50,000 gave about 5 percent. The statistics within Christian circles closely match these national averages.

Having said that, let me hasten to add that some Christians with sizable assets do give, and give mightily. For them the ability to make and give money is truly a gift from the Lord (notice what the Apostle Paul says about this gift of giving with liberality in Romans 12:8). For many Christians, making money (investing) is a logical extension of their spiritual gift (giving).

Some Christians rationalize retaining God's portion under the guise that they are saving it for future needs. This ruse can easily be detected because their current giving reflects a stingy spirit. Making more money won't encourage them to give more. Quite the contrary: It is more difficult to give out of more than it is out of less; those who have a million find it harder to give a tenth than those who have a thousand. The commitment to give must exist long before the funds are available.

As you make more money, through investing or laboring, there are more "opportunities" available to spend or reinvest it. I have known many Christians whose stated objectives were to invest more in order to give more. Most of those who reinvested God's portion ultimately lost it or spent it.

I'm sure that over the centuries there have been many Christians who used their talents to make and give money. Perhaps the best known of the twentieth century was R.G. LeTourneau, the inventor of most of the large road grading equipment used today. I would recommend to anyone who desires to see an example of the gift of giving that they read his biography, *Mover of Men and Mountains* (Moody Press, 1979).

To be honest, I know of very few Christians who invest primarily for the purpose of furthering their giving. Most make their money by investing and then feel a conviction to give from the surplus. It is really a shame that more Christians don't understand (and practice) the sowing and reaping principle Jesus taught in Luke 6:38, "Give, and it will be given to you; good measure, pressed down, shaken together, running over, they will pour into your lap. For by your standard of measure it will be measured to you in return." Note in this passage that Christ said *they* (men) will give back to those who give to God.

Of all the people I have personally counseled I have known only one who planned an investment strategy from the very beginning specifically to be able to give more to God's work. She is a widow whose husband operated a very profitable business. During his lifetime they developed a habit of giving large amounts of money to missionaries. After his death she desired to continue to give as they had previously, but since her husband had a buy-sell agreement with his partner she could only give out of the proceeds from the sale of the business. Within a year she realized that it would only be a short time, a few years at most, until she exhausted the funds from the sale and would no longer be able to give at their previous level; so she made a conscious decision to invest her surplus from the sale of the business and give away the profits.

She attended several classes on stock market investing and then set out on a plan to multiply her assets. I believe the Lord honored her heart attitude. She happened upon a small company that was just getting started in the medical field, and invested most of her resources in their stock. Within three years her assets had grown by more than 2,000 percent! She was able to continue her giving goals and, as best I know, continues to do so today.

By the way, she took all but a fraction of the stock and transferred it to a more conservative investment program once it had multiplied. When I asked her why, she said, "There is no sense in taking foolish risks. I have enough to give what we had been giving. Now I'll protect it."

Motive #2: Meeting Future Needs

In 2 Corinthians 12:14 Paul stated an accepted doctrine in his generation: that parents should store up for their children, not the children for their parents. It would seem that we have almost inverted that principle today. Children wonder how they are going to be able to care for their parents in their old age. Some of the problem is culture-related. Today it is considered acceptable to commit older family members to nursing homes, even if they are still able to live useful lives in a family environment. To a large extent this is simply a reflection of our selfish attitudes. We don't want to be inconvenienced by the care of older family, so it's easier to park them in constant care facilities. Obviously this is not true with all the elderly in nursing homes, but all too often it is.

Unfortunately, the net result is a much higher cost of care for aging parents (as well as depriving the younger generation of contact with their elders). I am aware that many exceptions exist. Aging family members with specific problems, such as Alzheimer's disease, need special medical help. But no one will ever convince me that the millions of aging parents now kept in nursing homes in the U.S. are all exceptions. Many, if not most, are indigent and are being supported through public funds. They failed to plan properly themselves and since welfare won't pay to keep them at home it is easier to place them in high-cost care facilities at the taxpayers' expense.

Providing for future needs includes areas such as education, retirement, travel, and possible unemployment. I would like to take a closer look at the first two of these.

THE HIGH COST OF EDUCATION

We have developed into a society where future success is tied almost directly to education. It is not that higher education in itself is necessary for success, except in the case of specific disciplines such as law or medicine. It is that a college educa tion is perceived as a need and is a criterion for a start in the business world. In other words, as more and more business owners and managers have become college graduates themselves, they have raised the entrance standards for potential managerial level employees to at least a college education.

As a result, most parents now perceive a college education for their children as a necessity of life. With the costs of education rising much faster than the economy as a whole, there are few alternatives except to invest to meet this need (perceived or real) or force both parent and child into long-term debt. The degree of risk an investor must assume is directly proportional to how much surplus is available currently and in the future.

Allow me to illustrate: If the cost of a college education at a state university is presently $50,000, and you have that much to put aside as a lump sum, your goal should be to keep the value of the money growing to match the rising cost of education, plus inflation.

This can be done in a variety of ways: You can prepay the tuition costs at a state university. This guarantees at least that the tuition expense will remain current, regardless of the economy. This also assumes the university will not default on its future contracts. The additional funds needed for room and board need only stay even with the general economy's inflation. Usually this can be accomplished by investing in good quality mutual funds that are widely diverse in their investments.

Other investments that can be used to help defray the cost of a college education are Series EE savings bonds that are tax exempt when used for education; zero coupon bonds, many of which are tax deferred until maturity; and even many retirement accounts, such as IRAs and 401Ks, that can be utilized for education needs without the normal tax penalties being applied.

Let's look at a more likely scenario. You can put some money aside to help with your children's education, but not enough to pay the entire costs. Then both your investment strategy and your children's expectations must be modified.

Your investment strategy must be more aggressive in order to meet the goal. Instead of investing in savings bonds or zero coupon bonds you must seek out higher risk investments that cannot only stay even with inflation, but grow to meet the need of inadequate savings.

In addition you will probably need to condition your children to attending a good community college for the first two years, and saving toward their own education costs. I personally believe this is a very good idea for Christian parents anyway. Usually when children are involved with paying some of the costs of an education they appreciate it more and apply themselves better. I realize that not every child is the same. Some apply themselves thoroughly even though their parents pay the entire costs. But in my counseling I have found that group to be in the minority. Usually those who pay some of their own costs and manage their own funds understand and appreciate their education more. I rather suspect thousands of Christian young people are in college on their parents' money just to delay making a decision about what they want to do with their lives for four more years.

If you have any doubt about the wisdom of disciplining your children rather than indulging them, just read the following verses sometime—Proverbs 6:20, 10:1, 12:1, 13:1, and 13:18. I find it is much easier to allow God's Word to do the convicting.

Not long ago I had a friend call to say that he had achieved his goal of providing college educations for his children. I had first met him in 1979 when he and his wife came in for budget counseling. They were not overspending, but realized they would never meet their goals for educating their two children on their present course. They were able to put aside about $50 a month toward education, after paying for private secondary schooling. The $600 a year they were saving, even at 10 percent interest a year, would not cover the costs of college educations for two children, ages six and eight.

We discussed several possible moves they could make, including some high-risk investments that might or might not succeed. After two sessions it was clear that high-risk investing was not for them. The thought of having all their children's college money at risk for 8 to 10 years did not fit either of their temperaments.

Since the mother was working primarily to meet the current educational expenses of their children in a private school and to be able to put something aside for college, I asked if they had considered home schooling their children. The mother was a primary school teacher and initially resisted the idea of home schooling. But after reading some literature on the growing home-schooling movement and the high scholastic rating most home schooled children achieved, they decided to try it. With the cost of private schooling removed, they actually netted an additional $50 a month to invest for college. Virtually all the income the wife had been earning had been consumed in education costs, child care, transportation, clothes, etc.

They took her teacher's retirement lump sum of approximately $3,000 and the $100 a month they could save and began to invest it. The investments they chose were tax certificates. Twice each year the county government where they lived auctioned off delinquent taxes in the form of certificates. These certificates paid an average of 18 percent interest (depending on the economy) with virtually no risk. If the taxes and interest were not paid within three years, the tax certificate purchasers owned the property on which taxes were due.

They followed this plan successfully for nearly 15 years without a single default. By the time their first child was ready for college they had accumulated nearly $80,000. They had achieved their education goals without the wife working, and each of their children qualified for full scholarships. Because of the scholarships, their children completed college with nearly $30,000 each to start their own families. This couple matched their personalities to their goals and their investment strategy.

Not long ago a well-known private university in Atlanta announced an innovative method of financing a college education at their institution. All it required was the parents and student to sign a 10-year promissory note with monthly payments of $917 for 120 months (10 years). The idea of parents pledging their home and all other possessions against a college loan of this magnitude is ridiculous. The belief that a college graduate with a bachelor's degree can repay such a loan is the height of assumption, in my opinion.

THE OPTION OF RETIREMENT

As I said previously, we seem to cycle from one extreme to another in our society today. Some people seem obsessed with retirement planning; they divert funds from God's work and their families and live like misers most of their lives in order to retire in "comfort."

Others act as if they will remain young and highly employable for the rest of their lives. With few exceptions, this attitude is very naive. Often they will end up living on inadequate income, mostly Social Security, or being totally dependent on their children.

In searching for the biblical principle of retirement I found there were very few references on the subject. In fact there is only one direct reference, and it is found in Numbers 8:25, "But at the age of 50 years they [the Levites] shall retire from service in the work and not work any more." Exactly why a temple priest was required to retire at 50 years of age, or what he did from that point on, is not clear. Taking the totality of Scripture in context we can assume that he had other duties to perform.

I interpret two fundamental points about retirement from

God's Word. First, we focus too much on ceasing our work at too early an age. Second, since most of us will not have the same income earning ability at 65 or 70, we need to lay aside some surpluses in our higher income years for use at a later time. Proverbs 6:6-8 describes the prudence of planning for the lean years. And Proverbs 21:20 tells us that a prudent man stores some of what he accumulates.

I believe the best retirement investment that anyone can make is to pay his home off as soon as possible. As noted earlier, with rare exception it is better to use the potential surplus funds that would go into a retirement account to pay off your home mortgage first, and then use the payments that you were making on the mortgage to start a retirement account.

I understand all the arguments about the money in a qualified retirement account being tax deferred, and the interest on a home mortgage being tax deductible. Even so, paying off your home mortgage first still makes more economic sense.

The additional benefit of knowing that your home belongs to you and not some mortgage company is worth it even if it costs more. If you don't believe that, just ask anyone who lost his home in a bad economy. I know hundreds of families who have paid off their homes in lieu of beginning an early retirement plan. Not one that I have ever talked to regretted it.

It is another conviction of mine, having observed many families, that most retirement plans should begin at about age 40. Sooner than that and the average investor sacrifices basic needs. I also doubt that anyone has the insight to look more than 30 years ahead in our current economy and accurately project what will be needed at retirement. But on the other hand, waiting to start a retirement program much beyond 40 usually requires too much risk to meet even reasonable goals.

Without a doubt the vast majority of professionals who have retirement plans would be better off if they simply parked their money in low-risk investments, rather than aim for the highest return. It's that same old basic principle: If you can generate the money to meet your goals, why take risks trying to multiply it?

The fundamental principle in any long-range financial planning is to develop a strategy that will meet your goals and stick to it. To do so successfully requires that some critical factors such as personality, age, and income be factored into your planning. We will look at these in the next chapter.

8

Critical Factors

There are many strategies for investing; no one of them is better or worse than the others. In great part the strategy you select depends on your goals, your age, your income, and your temperament. Each investor must consider all of these or the result will usually be turmoil, frustration, and financial loss.

For instance, I have a close friend who invests in basic metals such as lead, zinc, cobalt, and magnesium. In some cases he simply brokers the metals by locating one party who has a need and another who has a surplus. As a result, he reaps a reward by way of a commission. But there are instances where he is offered a good deal on a load of metals without being able to locate an immediate buyer. Then he must buy the product, store it until he can locate a willing buyer, and hope that the price goes up instead of down in the meantime.

Often he will have hundreds of thousands of dollars, equaling his total net worth, at risk in a particular metal. For him, just as for the commodities trader I discussed earlier, the risk of losing everything must fit his temperament. He has goals for retirement, education, giving, and remaining debt-free, just as we all should. But unless he were able to sleep at night, all the other goals would be meaningless. I can tell you that my basic temperament would not allow me to do the same kind of investing. Certainly anyone would like to reap the financial rewards he is able to achieve, but few people could accept the risks.

On the other hand, I am reminded of a counselee who inherited over a million dollars and was so fearful of losing it that she kept it in a passbook savings account at her local bank. The thought of being such a poor steward of those assets would force me to seek out a higher rate of return if the money were mine. I know that hundreds of missionaries could be sent and thousands of families could be fed out of the increase in her assets just by shifting to T-bills, CDs, or tax certificates with virtually no higher degree of risk.

It is therefore important to remember that strategy involves a great deal more than just achieving specific goals. It involves personality and temperament to a large degree. However, often our personalities and temperaments have flaws that would keep us from achieving God's full potential for our finances. To offset these flaws, God, in His infinite wisdom, has given most of us spouses who mirror ourselves. In other words, they are exact opposites I have said many times what I believe to be absolutely true: If a husband and wife are similar, one of them is unnecessary. In order to reach the proper balance in any investment strategy it is necessary that spouses communi cate regularly about finances. For those who are single through choice, divorce, or a spouse's death, it is important to seek out someone close (who is as opposite as possible) to act as a counselor. One of the ways you can tell when you have found the right person is that he or she is the one individual who never agrees with you.

THE COMMUNICATIONS FACTOR

With some exceptions men are the primary risk-takers in the area of investments. Perhaps this is by culture, or perhaps it is by temperament, but no matter the reason it is normally so. For instance, a man often looks at a house as a potential source of capital when needed. A woman looks at a house as her home and rarely is willing to risk it unless there is no other choice.

Men are far more subject to get-rich-quick schemes than are women. In fact, of the several hundred schemes I have personally known about, less than 5 percent were promoted or purchased by women. Perhaps this is because women have been conditioned to listen rather than react, and as a result they are better able to hear the Holy Spirit's voice warning them.

This I do know: I have sat across the table from scores of men who were describing some of the most incredibly stupid investment schemes I had ever heard of, most of which could be eliminated on the basis of common sense. Without any discussion I would often ask the wife, "What do you think about this idea?"

Her response was invariably the same. "I don't know what he's talking about, but I have a real check in my spirit about this."

With no real statistical information the wife usually came to the correct conclusion. It was as if God were saying to her, "Would you please stop this dummy before he loses any more money!"

Interestingly enough, though, if a husband is in financial need because of a bad decision and asks for his wife's help, I find most wives ready and willing to do whatever is necessary, including selling their homes, cars, jewelry, or other prized possessions.

Perhaps the verse that best describes the relationship that a husband and wife should have in all areas, including investing, is found in Genesis 2:24, "For this cause a man shall leave his father and his mother, and shall cleave to his wife; and they shall become one flesh." The closest translation to "one flesh" we have in our generation is "one person." God desires that a husband and wife function as one person, the strengths of one balancing the weaknesses of the other. One of the biggest mistakes any husband can make is to exclude his "helpmate" from the decision process. The same can be said of a wife, but for a wife to exclude her husband from financial decisions is uncommon.

Unfortunately, many wives don't want to be involved in the financial decisions of their husbands. This is very shortsighted on their part and denies the husband the balance God provides through the marriage relationship. It should also be noted that wives outlive their husbands nearly 85 percent of the time, the average age at which a woman is widowed being under 60 years of age. This means that most wives will end up inheriting their husbands' plans, whether they want to or not.

THE AGE FACTOR

Age is a very critical factor when making investment decisions. The younger you are, the more risk you can take and still recover if you're wrong. A 25-year-old investor can make some mistakes and still have plenty of time to recover. A 75-year-old investor can ill afford any mistakes, assuming he doesn't have an unlimited supply of money. And as I noted earlier, even $5 billion wasn't enough cushion for the Hunt brothers.

If you do not violate the principles of leverage and surety discussed earlier in this book, there are virtually no situations from which you cannot recover if you are 40 years of age or less. The most you can lose is the money you have at risk. And assuming you didn't borrow it you can only lose what you have, not future earnings. Therefore it would seem reasonable to expect younger investors to be more of the risk-takers, assuming again that they have the temperament to accept some losses.

Several years ago a young man called to ask for counseling. He was interested in investing in commodity option contracts and was trying to do what the Bible admonished in terms of seeking counsel from older Christians.

As you have probably gathered by now, I am not a great

advocate of commodities investing since much of it borders on pure gambling. In a conversation over lunch this young man described the research he had done on a particular commodity (wheat) and the prospect of an extremely poor wheat crop in the Soviet Union that year. He was considering buying some options on winter wheat futures. By buying an option his loss would be limited only to the money he had at risk. If the wheat prices went down he could forfeit his option, losing what he had invested to that point but with no contingent liability. If prices went up he could execute his option and sell the wheat or actually resell his option at a profit.

He had saved the money he wanted to risk and had discussed the idea with his wife, who had agreed to support whatever decision he made. They had no children and were renting an apartment. If his "hunch" was right he could make enough money to buy a home for cash, lay aside several thousand dollars for future education needs, and still have several thousand dollars left over.

My question to him was, "If you lost every dime you plan to risk, would you look back with regret?"

He said he had prayed about it and felt he could accept either the loss or gain as the Lord's will.

"What about your wife?" I asked.

"She feels the same way," he replied without hesitation.

"Then go for it," I told him. "If you don't, you may never have this chance again." Upon such opportunities are fortunes made (and lost).

He did purchase the options for winter wheat. That year Russia suffered its largest crop loss in nearly a hundred years. The money he had risked grew by nearly 2,000 percent, at which time he cashed out, paid his tithes and taxes, bought a home for cash, and invested nearly $25,000 in a quality mutual fund for his future children's education. He never repeated the investment risk he took that year, to my knowledge, and settled into a career as a computer programmer. But at 25 he had time to recover, even if he had made a bad guess.

A doctor friend in his mid-thirties had made some poor investments in apartment buildings that created so much stress that they nearly wrecked his health and marriage. He correctly observed the principles of debt and surety by investing in limited partnerships that required only the commitment of his initial investment capital. However, the investments had outstanding mortgage loans. Several of the investments failed due to economic circumstances, creating a huge tax liability for him. Many of the investments he had made through his retirement plan also went sour, causing the IRS to do an audit. They determined that many of the loans and investments he had made violated the "prudent man rule" (taking a risk a prudent man would not take). They disallowed his retirement plan, throwing the previously deferred income into his taxable income. He ended up owing the IRS several hundred thousand dollars in taxes and penalties, plus interest.

A later appeal to the tax court overturned the IRS ruling and required only that he repay the retirement plan the lost earnings, which amounted to about $100,000. He also lost about $30,000 in legal and accounting fees.

Actually, this man was extremely fortunate, because only about 30 percent of tax court decisions go in favor of the taxpayers. By the time his case reached the court he was well into his forties and his income had declined substantially due to competition from HMOs in his area. Remember that anytime you are using tax-deferred money to invest (whether for retirement, government bonds, etc.) you are potentially extending the risk into a later time period. By the time your case works its way through the IRS and the courts, if necessary, you may be well past your youth.

Almost weekly on our call-in radio program, "Money Matters," someone will share a story of how he risked his life's savings and lost it. Usually these are people who were either retired or approaching retirement and realized that they hadn't accumulated enough assets for retirement. Realistically most people need about 75 to 80 percent of their preretirement income in order to retire. Since they do little investigation about what Social Security benefits will actually pay, they get a real shock at retirement. If they have received a lump sum from their company retirement plan they find themselves eating into the principal each month. This leads them to take risks at an age where the loss of virtually any assets cannot be replaced. Most people in this situation would be far better off to face the reality that they need to supplement their retirement by working, not taking investment risks.

The era of junk bonds in the early to mid-eighties yielded some investments with earnings of more than 20 percent a year. In an economy where CDs and T-bills were yielding 6 to 7 percent, this was just too much temptation for many older investors. Several retirees I know shifted their entire life savings into these high-yield bonds and bond funds. They beat the system for a while and earned double or triple the going conservative interest rates. In spite of any counsel to the contrary, those whom I knew refused to believe they could lose their money. After all, these investments were offered by some of the biggest brokerage firms in the world, and the companies backing the bonds were blue chip with ratings of AA or better.

There was really no way to convince them that the risk was too high. I wrote letters suggesting that they should withdraw the majority of their funds and secure them. I received angry calls and letters from brokers who even threatened lawsuits if I didn't quit maligning their products. I am not an investment analyst, but common sense and logic say you don't get something for nothing. If an investor is promised twice the average return that a normal bond is offering, he should probably assume there is at least twice the risk.

In the late eighties, reality struck home as many companies found themselves stuck with high-interest junk bonds in a declining economy. Most could not even maintain the interest payments. They apparently had assumed the good times would last forever, and had leveraged their companies up to and beyond their limits. Many of these companies simply filed for bankruptcy protection, leaving the junk bond holders with little or nothing. Even those that didn't file for bankruptcy "renegotiated" their bonds to reduce and delay the interest payments.

Not only did many banks, savings and loans, and insurance companies that held these bonds fail, but millions of smaller investors, Christians included, saw their assets dwindle to practically nothing.

I mention the junk bond era not because I believe junk bonds will again be offered to the average investor as a "good deal." They will not be; at least not in this generation. Too many people got burned and remember it too well. But junk bonds simply represent a class of investments that will always be available to the naive investor. These are investments that seem too good to be true, and are the darlings of the invest-ment brokers. In the sixties it was the high tech stocks, in the seventies it was land syndications, in the eighties it was junk bonds and tax shelters. In the nineties it will be something else, and on into the next century it will be still another deal too good to be true.

Just remember, the older you are and the greater your need for excessive returns, the more susceptible you are to these schemes.

THE INCOME FACTOR

It seems to be a human fallacy that the more income people have at their disposal the less cautious they are with it. Some years ago I did an informal survey of some doctors and busi-ness owners I knew to determine how many of them had lost money in a bad investment. I was astounded to discover that 100 percent of those surveyed had made at least one bad investment.

Next I surveyed some middle-income families I had coun-seled and found out that about 50 percent of them had lost money in a bad investment.

Finally, I surveyed average-income families. Of this group about 10 percent had lost money through a bad investment.

The logical conclusion you could draw is that those in the lower income group had less money to risk so they obviously would have made fewer investments. Not so. The percentage of investments made stayed remarkably constant, regardless of the income. But the kinds of investments they chose and risks they assumed changed drastically depending on their incomes.

My conclusion is that the lower income investors are less willing to assume high risks. The higher income investors willingly accept the greater risks. Probably much of this can be explained by what is called "sweat equity." In other words, the lower the income the more sweat went into the money to be risked.

Perhaps the lesson to be learned from this survey is: Treat all of your money as if you earned it chopping firewood for a living.

9

Where to Go for Advice

O ne of the most common questions I am asked is, "Where can I go to get good investment advice?" The answer to that can range all the way from an inexpensive magazine or newsletter to very expensive professional counsel. There is no "right" answer to the question. In large part it depends on the same factors we just discussed: age, income, and temperament.

BUDGETING

Perhaps the best way to address the subject of where to go for advice is to start with the basics and work our way up.

The first tier or level in seeking advice is to be able to manage the money you earn in order to create a surplus to invest. In the simplest of terms this is called budgeting. Everyone needs a budget, even those with higher incomes. It is impossible to be a good steward of what God has entrusted to you if you don't manage it well. Obviously those with less income also need budgets or they will never develop a surplus that can be multiplied.

I have written extensively on the subject of budgeting and therefore will not occupy more space in this book to repeat it. For more detailed information refer to *The Financial Planning Workbook* (Moody Press) or *The Complete Financial Guide for*

Young Couples (Victor Books), available at most Christian bookstores. Both contain step-by-step instructions as well as the forms necessary to budget one year of income and expenses.

Any good budget should be no more complicated than is absolutely necessary to manage your finances. It must be developed by both the husband and wife together. And it must be fair and balanced, not abusive.

To develop a working budget should take about four hours of planning and no more than 30 minutes per pay period to maintain. Any more than that and it's too complicated. A great many people are now using some form of computerized budgeting system on a home computer; some excellent software programs are available for less than $100. I personally don't use one yet because I can maintain my home budget faster manually. When the systems are advanced enough to pay bills by direct computer access I will probably convert to an automated system.

For those who need personalized help in developing and managing a budget, there are thousands of trained volunteers who provide this counsel in their communities and churches all across the U.S. To locate one in your area, consult the counselor referral section in the Appendix. For those who have debt problems, a national nonprofit organization called the Consumer Credit Counseling Service has affiliate offices in almost every major city in the country.

Remember this principle because it is a fundamental one that I will refer to often as we evaluate various investments later: The best investment you will ever make is debt reduction. Each dollar of credit card debt you reduce is the equivalent of making a guaranteed investment at 18 to 21 percent. You'll have a very difficult time matching that return.

The return for paying off car loans may not be quite as good. They often average only 12 to 14 percent. Try to find a guaranteed investment with an equivalent return.

The return for paying off home mortgage loans may drop as

low as 9 percent for some families. That is still a good return with no risk. And remember that if you pay off your home, *you* own it, not a mortgage company. No matter how bad the economy gets no one will be able to force you out of your own home.

ADVISORS FOR ENTRY-LEVEL INVESTORS

Once you have a workable budget and develop a surplus to invest, learn as much as you can before taking any risks. Usually the counselors or advisors available to low-budget investors are commissioned salespeople who make their livings by selling products such as insurance, mutual funds, and annuities. This is not an indictment against these salespeople. In practical truth a professional investment advisor cannot make a living selling financial planning services to this level of investor. The fee-only planner would have to charge several hundred dollars and could do little, if any, follow-up.

So it means that a low-budget investor has three basic options: (1) do your own investing and pay the price of learning as you go; (2) take the advice of the product salesman and hope that he or she sells a good quality product; (3) seek out inexpensive written materials that you can rely on for guidance.

Since the first two alternatives are self-explanatory, I will concentrate on the third: materials.

A variety of good materials is available to help and advise nonprofessional investors. Several of these are listed in the resource section in the Appendix. Usually first-time investors subscribe to too many resources. This often results in confusion and frustration because often one publication will contradict another. The key is to select resources that don't push a particular agenda such as precious metals, insurance, mutual funds, and the like. I personally prefer magazines that don't accept advertising from investment product sales companies. I think it would be very difficult as an editor to be objective if you knew that a sizable portion of your revenue came from a product you were evaluating.

Newsletters are generally a good source of basic advice. There are some 1,700 financial newsletters published in the United States. Some are free; most carry subscription rates of up to several hundred dollars a year. They range all the way from general economic information to detailed analysis of specific investments, such as stocks, bonds, real estate, and mutual funds.

I recommend that low-budget or first-time investors subscribe to newsletters written specifically for them. Again, the key is to verify if the editors have a hidden (or sometimes not so hidden) agenda. It is also crucial to verify the track record of the managing editor since usually that person is the primary advice giver.

One popular newsletter writer I have observed for several years promotes a doom and gloom message (which is easy to sell in a bad economy). He advises his followers to buy guns, gold, and food for the coming collapse, the same basic message he has promoted for nearly 30 years. (He gained great popularity after the run-up in gold prices in the late seventies.) What most of his readers don't know is that his success as an investment advisor came right on the heels of several complete financial failures for him personally. His single success—predicting gold prices would escalate after the ownership of gold was again legalized for Americans—was a one-time fluke. His subsequent success record on investment advice has been about 12 percent. You can do better than that by flipping a coin and save yourself about $300 a year in newsletter costs.

Look for a newsletter that takes the first-time investor through each phase of learning, including *specific* advice about what investments to use at each level of income and assets. While no one source should be used to the exclusion of all others, I recommend newsletters as a good first resource.

A noncommercial magazine which has developed a high level of integrity over the years is *Consumer Reports.* The credibility of the magazine is based on accepting no advertising from any source, and the fact that they purchase all the products they evaluate. Once a year the magazine does an analysis of insurance, mutual funds, and a variety of other financial products. It is well worth the time and cost to invest in these issues and study them carefully before starting an investment program.

A second magazine I recommend is *Money Magazine.* Although more commercial in nature than *Consumer Reports, Money* has excellent information about mutual funds, insurance investments, and the like.

Beyond these resources I personally don't rely on much that is printed besides the normal daily reports such as *The Wall Street Journal* and *Investor's Daily.* I'm sure there are other sources that many of you use regularly, and I have listed some of the more well-known ones in the Appendix. But with limited time I try to limit myself to only those I can scan quickly.

THE COMMISSIONED SALESMAN

The next tier up in investment advice is using someone who sells a product (or products) and generates a commission (as opposed to charging a fee).

I have to be honest and say that my observations of this type of investment counselor have been mixed. There are many men and women who are very qualified to give good, objective counsel and also earn commissions in the process. But the industry is also full of novices or incompetents who sell only what they have been taught to sell and offer little or no balance in their advice. One way to sort them out is to require several references from others with whom they have worked. I recommend checking with at least five of their clients to verify their track record. It is also important that these people have been clients for at least three years. If they won't provide the references, I suggest that you keep on looking. At the very best, selecting the proper investments can be both frustrating and confusing. What you don't need is a salesman making it worse by giving misinformation.

Unfortunately, many of these salespeople stretch the truth a lot in order to make a sale. They represent their products as high-yield and secure, when in truth many are low-yield and highly risky. Let me use an example: A man who came to me for counsel had been sold an insurance policy as a good investment, as well as lifetime protection for his family. The salesman presented the plan as a guaranteed 9 percent return. The concept behind the policy was that once the premiums had been paid for a period of six years no further contributions would be required and the dividends would compound at 9 percent a year for life. The salesman even presented computer printouts reflecting this return ("With no risk," he said).

Later, the buyer discovered that the returns the salesman quoted were based on the gross earnings of the insurance company. After the service fees, commissions, and administrative expenses were deducted, the actual earnings were less than 6 percent.

The policy would, at best, require 10 years of payments to be fully funded. Unfortunately the company's earnings declined over the next few years and the payment period grew to nearly 15 years. After four years of payments the buyer had virtually no accumulated value in the policy, except the cash values, which belonged to the insurance company and would become loans against the policy if he drew them out.

His "investment advisor" was a new hire who had lost his job in industry and had chosen insurance sales (investment advising) by default. He didn't purposely lie. He simply didn't know enough to discern the truth.

My advice when selecting a commissioned sales person is: Be certain he or she has at least a five-year track record in the industry. I have said this before and have received angry letters from advisors who are new in the field. Their common argument is, "How will we ever get the experience if people won't use us until we're seasoned by at least five years of experience?"

My answer is, "Sell to your family and close friends and be extremely cautious about what you don't know during this learning phase. Then verify the track records of other agents in your company and see if what you have been taught is right. If not, change companies until you find a good one."

Let me repeat again, many good, honest, ethical salespeople are to be found in the financial field. But they are the ones who think more about their clients than they do their own financial needs. A hungry agent will often oversell, pressure, and prod a client. Those who try to put a guilt trip on you to buy from them because they are Christians (or church members) should be avoided with all diligence. If an agent's products and track record will not stand by themselves—stay away. Otherwise you'll probably lose your money as well as a friend.

One last note on this point: Perhaps the worst of these salespeople are the doom-and-gloomers who sell "collapse-proof" investments such as gold and silver. Several investment groups have taken to using the Christian media, particularly radio, to ply their wares. They use guests who speak of a coming worldwide economic disaster (perhaps true) and then tout precious metals as the protector of all real wealth. Too often they quote, or misquote, Old Testament passages such as Haggai 2:8, " 'The silver is Mine, and the gold is Mine,' declares the Lord of hosts," as justification for buying their products. My counsel is: Avoid these "prophets" of doom who actually have in mind their own "profits."

FEE-PLUS-COMMISSION ADVISORS

In addition to advisors who make their incomes exclusively from commission sales, there are a growing number of investment advisors who will work either way—fees or commission sales, or both. Usually these advisors will initially provide counsel for a fixed fee per hour. Then if you elect to buy products from them they will reduce the fee by the commissions they receive.

A prudent investor would do well to remember that a counselor or advisor usually exercises an undue influence over his or her clients. In many instances this means investors end up buying what the advisors recommend, which are usually the products they sell. The question then becomes, is the fee-plus-commission really a ploy to get clients to buy from them while thinking they are receiving objective advice? That totally depends on the character of the advisor, something you will need to discern for yourself. A simple comparison of the value and prices of the products suggested will tell you whether or not the counselor is totally objective. If the investment products they offer are as good as those offered through other agents, then why not buy from them and reduce the fees? But if what they offer is inferior or higher priced, avoid the advice as well as the product.

FEE-ONLY INVESTMENT ADVISORS

A fee-only advisor is exactly what the name implies. He or she charges a fee, but does not sell any products or accept commissions—usually. I say "usually" because I have found some advisors who advertised themselves as fee-only planners but accepted commissions, known as "finders' fees," from product companies. In my opinion this is blatantly dishonest and I would avoid advisors who do this.

By virtue of the fact that they generate their income from fees, you can expect fee-only advisors to be expensive. Most cater to the upper-income investor and often have a minimum level of net worth for the clients they advise. The fees can range from several hundred dollars for a one-time evaluation to several thousand a year for continuing clients.

In general I have not found fee-only advisors to be any more accurate in their advice than a well-seasoned, fee-plus-commission advisor, although there are exceptions.

The one area where fee-only planners usually excel is in designing long-term investment strategies for their clients. Since follow-up is so essential they also usually do a good job at getting their clients to implement their plans. After all, if you're paying someone $10,000 a year to advise you, you'll usually do what they say.

Fee-only planners run the gamut from conservative to speculative just as do those who earn commissions. You will need to select a planner based on your personality and objectives. But since they do cater to upper-income clients with sizable asset portfolios, the logical perspective should be preservation of capital, rather than speculation.

Of the professional investment advisors I queried about fee versus non-fee planners, the assessments were split nearly down the middle. I have attempted to provide an objective evaluation of both the good and bad sides of fee versus commission advisors. But the single most consistent comment offered by virtually all the advisors I asked was, "Check out their track record carefully."

The bottom line of any investment advisor is not whether you paid their salaries by way of a fee or a commission. It is whether they made you more money than they cost you. A commissioned salesman who makes his clients 12 percent after all commissions, administrative charges, and market fluctuations are taken into account is still better than a fee-only planner who makes his clients 6 percent after all costs.

Remember to ask for at least five local references that you can talk with about your advisor's track record. If you can't get them to share such a list with you, keep on looking.

CHRISTIAN OR NON-CHRISTIAN ADVISORS?

Psalm 1:1-2 says, "How blessed is the man who does not walk in the counsel of the wicked, nor stand in the path of sinners, nor sit in the seat of scoffers! But his delight is in the law of the Lord, and in His law he meditates day and night." There is a clear implication here that our primary source of counsel should be from those who know the Lord. Does this imply that we should never take counsel from an unbeliever? I don't think so. I believe the implication is not to rely on secular counsel as our daily source of wisdom. All counsel should be weighed against the wisdom of God's Word and discarded if it fails the test. That includes Christian and non-Christian counsel.

Put in perspective, I would say to any Christian, seek out the best Christian investment counsel available to you. But if it is not adequate, as is too often the case, then seek out the counsel of knowledgeable, ethical nonbelievers. Just be sure to weigh their counsel against the wisdom in God's Word.

Some time back I needed angioplasty surgery on one of the arteries to my heart. I called a cardiologist friend at an excellent hospital in Atlanta and asked who he thought was the best angioplastyst at his hospital. Without hesitation he gave me the name of the cardiologist he would use himself if he were having the same procedure done. As it turned out, the doctor was a Christian also and I felt a great relief when he accepted me as a patient.

But the actual specialist my cardiologist used to perform the delicate procedure was not a Christian. My friend's comment was, "He is the best in the world at this particular procedure. I believe God would want you to have the best."

I agreed, and he did the procedure successfully. The point is, I used Christians as my primary counsel, but used the best technicians to actually perform the procedure. As a Christian you will need to settle this issue of Christian and non-Christian counsel yourself.

Personally I would rather have a competent nonbeliever (as long as our basic values were compatible) than an incompetent believer who would give me bad advice. Let me assure you, I have known several investment advisors who memorized a lot of Scripture but didn't know their trade very well. Proverbs 14:7 applies to Christians and non-Christians alike: "Leave the presence of a fool, or you will not discern words of knowledge."

WHERE TO FIND
GOOD INVESTMENT ADVISORS

This is another one of those difficult questions for which there is no absolute answer. Many people call our offices asking if we recommend any particular advisors. Our answer is always a resounding no!

We have trained many financial counselors who help people with their budgets, and teach the biblical principles of handling money, usually within their own churches. If we hear that one of our volunteer counselors is giving investment advice to those they counsel, we remove that person from our recommended list. We are here to advise people how to manage their finances, not where to invest.

But since many people need good investment advice also, I would like to offer some advice on locating a good advisor.

1. *Ask around in your church and Bible studies for references.* Don't hesitate to ask if the advisor has made them money over the years. Also apply the five-year rule (10 if possible). Anyone can guess right one time, and one guess does not establish a track record. If a counselor has not ridden out at least one major recession in his field, in my opinion he is still a novice.

2. *Check his credentials with the National Association of Securities Dealers, if he is a registered broker.* If he has ever had his license suspended or revoked, be very cautious.

3. *Ask several local accountants who do tax returns for people you know.* Often they see the good and the bad of a planner's efforts. Although most will hesitate to give a negative report on someone, most will not hesitate to give a positive report on the good ones. If the accountant uses a financial planner because of how well he or she has done for one of the accountant's clients, that is a very strong recommendation.

DISCOUNT BROKERS

Over the last decade or so, many discount brokerage firms have been started that will place investment orders for very low commissions. This trend is certain to grow as banks expand further into the investment area. These firms cannot offer investment counsel to their clients. They are restricted to placing the buy or sell orders issued by their clients. Once you have a level of expertise that allows you the freedom to make your own investment decisions, the use of a discount broker can save you a great deal of money when trading.

10

Following Solomon's Advice

T here is no doubt that if I were looking for investment advice I would go to the person who had the best track record with his own money. I have a friend who is particularly good at selecting profitable investments. For several years he has allowed some missionaries to invest some of their meager earnings in many of his ventures. Thus far his success rate has been almost 100 percent. Sometimes the investments only make a little, sometimes a lot. But they have always been on the positive side. Most investors wish they could say as much for those times when they have chosen their own investments. It would be ridiculous for the missionaries who invest with my friend to launch out on their own. After all, he offers proven and tested counsel at no cost.

Few people realize that another investment counselor also does this. The best investor the world has ever known (outside of the Lord, obviously) was King Solomon. The Queen of Sheba noted that everything his hands touched prospered. So it would seem logical that if we could glean some investment advice from him we should be able to improve our percentages too. Fortunately, Solomon talked a great deal about his financial philosophies, as well as many other areas of life. The Lord told Solomon that He would endow him with riches, honor, and wisdom. Over the centuries he has been noted as the wisest man who ever lived (again outside of our Lord).

There are two basic investment principles Solomon discussed in the Book of Ecclesiastes and one in the Book of Proverbs that are worth our attention.

INVESTMENT PRINCIPLE #1:
DIVERSIFICATION

Solomon wrote in Ecclesiastes 11:2, "Divide your portion to seven, or even to eight, for you do not know what misfortune may occur on the earth." I interpret this to mean that we should divide our wealth (investment capital) into several parts and not risk it all in one place. This concept was known in prior generations as, "Don't put all your eggs in one basket."

Diversification is essential regardless of your age, income level, time frame, or personality. Obviously those with small amounts of money to invest cannot diversify as well as those with greater resources. But as your savings grow, your diversity should grow too.

It is important to diversify not only into different investments, but also into differing areas of the economy. Usually certain types of investments move inversely as the economy cycles. For example, when interest rates go up, fixed income investments such as current issue bonds go up too, while common stocks trend downward.

When the stock market is doing well and investor confidence is high, generally precious metals are down. Obviously there are always going to be individual exceptions caused by outside circumstances such as war, pestilence, and earthquakes. And there are times when it seems that contrary investments are moving in unison, but these are anomalies, caused in part by the complexities of our manipulated economy. Sometimes contrary investments are actually crossing the same threshold, with one heading up and the other heading down.

And, lest we forget that investing is an art and not a science, it is important to remember that people, their decisions, and their emotions affect the movements of investments. For instance, decisions by the Federal Reserve Board can affect the money supply and interest rates regardless of what is happening in the "real" economy. So short-term rates might be increasing at the same time long-term rates are dropping.

A good example that investing is more art than science can be seen in the great bull market of early 1991. Several thousand "program" traders (those who buy and sell based on computer models) received clear signals that the stock market would decline. This was a thoroughly logical analysis of an economy in recession and a pending war in the Persian Gulf. Thousands of these hearty speculators sold "short," meaning they borrowed stocks at current prices hoping to repay them at a future date with cheaper stocks as the prices fell.

Unfortunately, prices didn't fall. They rose rapidly and steadily for more than three months. Billions of dollars were lost by the program traders whose computers predicted higher oil prices, a sell-off in the stock market, and rising inflation. They missed on all three counts by several months.

But even though such exceptions occasionally occur, over the long run different investments move in opposite cycles. To avoid being wiped out if you need money during one of these cycles, diversity is essential. The principle is simple: Draw from the investments that are cyclically up and hold those that are down, and you won't get wiped out.

I have a friend who retired from dentistry with virtually all of his assets in good rental properties that had served him well for many years. Then, about two years into his retirement, his area of the country experienced a major recession lasting about three years, and many renters defaulted. Unable to live on the declining rental incomes, he was forced to sell some properties at substantial losses to generate income. Three years after he sold some of his rentals at distressed prices, the buyers resold the properties at nearly twice what he had received. He quickly diversified as the housing market in his area recovered.

In our ever changing economy, investors would be wise to diversify even into some foreign assets that are not subject to the swings in the U.S. economy. Certain mutual funds offer this kind of diversity.

When I discuss investment strategies for different ages of life later in this book, I will share some practical investments available to most average investors that offer a reasonable degree of diversity, but don't require a high degree of risk or expertise. Again, my basic philosophy is: I don't want to have to wake up every day wondering what brilliant moves I must make to protect my limited assets. If your goal is to maximize your profits (and risk), while maximizing your stress, you probably need to return this book for a refund and buy one on "no-money-down real estate," or "how to short the market and make a mint." I have known people who have attempted one or all of these. Some are in jail. Some are in hiding. And virtually all of them are dead broke.

In 1977 I met a retired couple who were living on the income from Sears department store stock. The husband had retired from Sears 10 years earlier after working his way up from a shoe clerk to department manager over some 40 years. During the Depression years, Sears had often paid their employees a portion of their incomes in stock, since they lacked the funds to pay in cash. As a result he had accumulated a significant amount of Sears stock, traditionally one of the best stocks in America since the Great Depression.

After retirement he and his wife were able to live quite well off the dividends and an interesting strategy of buying and selling some of his stocks annually. He had developed a strategy that was quite imaginative. Each year in the summer off-sale season, Sears stock would dip in value; then during the Christmas season it would regain its value. Knowing this, he would sell a portion of his stock in the winter, and repurchase it in the spring, often gleaning several thousand dollars profit to augment their income.

Not being emotionally attached to Sears, I suggested that he convert some of his stock and diversify into other areas that were not so single-purposed. But he and his wife had a strong loyalty to the company and forgot the cardinal rule of investing—objectivity. He couldn't bring himself to sell any of the stock permanently. "Besides," he said, "this plan has worked very well for nearly 10 years while many of our friends have lost money in their investments."

There was no way to argue that what he said was anything but correct. The only argument I had was that nothing is forever, except the Lord. Diversification does not guarantee success. But it does reduce the risks long-term.

When discount stores such as K Mart and Wal-Mart entered the retailing business they forever altered the way chains like Sears and J.C. Penney do business. Sears stock took some swift and terrible losses as a result. The last time I saw this couple their assets had dwindled to less than half of what they were previously, and both were forced to reenter the job market to supplement their incomes.

If you select mutual funds as your primary investment vehicle, they will usually offer a high degree of diversification within a single fund. For instance, most good funds allow investors to shift their money from an aggressive growth stock fund to a corporate bond or government fund without penalty at least once per year. If you are investing through a company retirement plan into a mutual fund you will normally have this same election at least once each year. Some funds even offer their investors the right to shift to another mutual fund entirely, such as their international fund, with only a small administrative fee. Obviously, asking about these options is an important part of selecting the right investment for your needs.

INVESTMENT PRINCIPLE #2:
ETHICAL INVESTING

The second principle taught by Solomon is found in Ecclesiastes 12:13, "The conclusion, when all has been heard, is: fear

God and keep His commandments, because this applies to every person." This certainly is good advice for anyone, but it is absolutely essential for Christians. Therefore, the first thought any Christian must have is, "Is what I am about to do going to be pleasing to the Lord?" If not, stay away from it— no matter what the potential profit.

Usually this comes under the heading of what is called "ethical" investing in our generation. There are investments that can yield very high rates of return with little or no risk. The difficulty is they prey off the weaknesses of others.

One example of this is a whiskey future. There are companies that specialize in selling whiskey futures, just as others do in real estate or corporate bonds. The concept is simple. When whiskey manufacturers brew their product it needs to be aged. Rather than leave their own money tied up in these barrels of whiskey, they sell (more like a lease) them to investors who hold the whiskey for the time required. Once it is properly aged, the whiskey company redeems the futures contract and markets the product. Often a whiskey future will yield from 3 to 5 percent higher return than other "safe" investments. Is it a good investment? No doubt about it. Is it honoring to the Lord? No doubt that it is not.

Similar types of investments can be found in many diverse industries.

Pharmaceutical companies that have holdings in foreign subsidiaries often sell abortives outside the United States to kill unborn children.

Some U.S. drug companies purposely overproduce drugs that are shipped to virtually unregulated countries and eventually make their way back into our country as street drugs.

I once had a friend who owned a considerable investment in Holiday Inns of America stock. The stock had done quite well and appeared to be heading for even higher levels. But after reading an article about Holiday Inns offering pornographic movies in their rooms my friend sold all of his stock and divested himself of any mutual funds that owned more than a fractional interest in the chain. He also wrote the corporate officers expressing his convictions.

One interesting side note about his decision is that shortly after he sold out his stock the law governing long-term capital gains was changed to disallow the 50-percent exclusion for stock held more than six months. If he had waited just one year more his taxes on the sale would have nearly doubled. The moral: It's profitable to listen to the Lord's convictions.

This issue of ethical investing is one that comes up often in our counseling. There are really two diverse opinions that any Christian needs to consider. The first is expressed by Amy Domini and Peter Kinder in their book, *Ethical Investing* (Addison-Wesley, 1984). Basically their perspective is that a Christian (or anyone else) should avoid any company, or mutual fund, that contains even a fractional interest in any product or industry that would be deemed socially unethical.

In principle I agree with their position. The difficulty arises in actually implementing it. If you buy into a mutual fund and observe their stock portfolio from year to year you will find that it changes significantly. The managers buy and sell frequently to take advantage of changing values. Unless the company has a clearly stated policy of what it will or will not invest in, you may find that they were "socially ethical" in one year and not in the next. The way to avoid this conflict is to buy and sell your own stocks, bonds, real estate, etc., and only select companies where the leadership adheres to your same ethical standards, which is virtually impossible. However, there are some mutual fund companies that strive to adhere to Judeo-Christian values. A newsletter called "The Social Investment Forum" tracks these companies on a regular basis. The address is listed in the Appendix.

The alternative opinion to never investing in any fund or company that has even an incidental interest in socially questionable areas is expressed by Austin Pryor, editor of the "Sound Mind Investor" newsletter. He also agrees that a Christian should never invest with any company that is blatantly unethical in its product philosophy. But of investments, such as mutual funds, that have only an incidental interest, he says:

> The average investor's interest would represent only 1/1000 of the fund's ownership. And the fund itself may represent only 1/1000 of the company's stock ownership. To divest yourself of the fund's stock does not hurt or influence the company's operations at all.

Instead, Pryor suggests that not buying a particular company's products may be a far more effective and practical way to influence their social ethics. Also he notes that if you own even one share of stock in a company with whose policies you disagree, you have the right to attend the annual stockholders' meetings and voice your opinion in public.

Both of the preceding arguments have validity and I will leave it to you to decide which is the right perspective for you.

In my experience I have found that boycotting a company's products has a much greater effect on their policies than boycotting their stock. I live in a relatively small community where the local convenience store was purchased by a national chain. Almost immediately they installed a rack of pornographic magazines. I took the time to get a comment form from the clerk, who also said she disagreed with the magazines. I wrote the parent company, and within two weeks received a letter of apology from the company president. A week later the magazines were removed. I doubt seriously if they would have responded in the same manner if I had simply threatened not to buy any stock in their company. But again, each of us has to make an individual choice.

INVESTMENT PRINCIPLE #3:
GOOD COUNSEL

The one last bit of direction I would offer from Solomon is the admonition that good counsel is essential to good planning. I made that point in an earlier chapter, but it is so important I would like to emphasize it one more time. As Proverbs 15:22 says, "Without consultation, plans are frustrated, but with many counselors they succeed."

One of my major frustrations is the contradicting counsel that is offered by investment advisors and financial planners who present themselves as experts. It's no wonder that many people either don't try to invest at all, or they simply park their money in low-interest savings accounts. Often they have listened to bad counsel and lost a lot of money, usually on the advice of another Christian

Most Christians don't want to give a bad report about another Christian, so even when someone asks for an opinion on the abilities or ethics of another Christian they hedge by saying, "Oh, he's a nice guy."

I have also done this in the past, to the detriment of some friends, and have purposed never to do so again. I will not give a bad report without first confronting the person involved, but I also won't skirt the question and allow someone else to suffer a loss that I could have prevented.

The example that always comes to mind is a Christian who left the insurance business to go into financial planning during the eighties. He passed all the licensing requirements, took the appropriate courses, and even learned the language well. But from the first time we met, through a mutual Christian friend, I knew he was a poor financial planner. He was a likable person, definitely a committed believer, but totally incompetent to give good investment advice.

He had been one of the top salesmen for a major insurance company and was a salesman personified. He made friends of virtually everyone he met, and was so likable they felt compelled to buy from him.

I knew that a friend was considering doing business with him, but rather than tell him my convictions I simply said, "Be sure you check it out with your accountant first." As I look back, that was just a cop-out to avoid what I assumed would be an unpleasant confrontation. Also I thought the accountant would realize the planner was incompetent too. Unfortunately, he didn't, or at least he didn't say so. Not only did my friend invest a sizable amount of money as a result of this planner's advice, but he also introduced the planner to several of his friends.

The investments the planner recommended were truly awful. They were a combination of tax shelters, limited partnerships, and low-quality insurance products. One of the worst was an ostrich ranch where these large, ornery birds were being promoted as the answer to the growing demand for low-fat meats (and an illusionary market for ostrich feathers). After a two-year attempt to create a "McOstrich" franchise the project was abandoned, along with several hundred thousand dollars of investors' money.

My friend, and his former friends, are still paying for this counselor's advice. They ended up owing the IRS taxes and penalties for the tax shelters that failed, including the ostrich ranch. The advisor has gone back to selling insurance and is doing quite well himself. I learned a lesson through this that has stuck with me: When you know the truth, say it (in love).

My counsel is, always use more than one advisor, including your spouse. Tell them to be as honest with you as they would want you to be if the roles were reversed.

11

The Financial
Seasons of Life:
Ages 20 to 40

I have often said that if I could go back and relive my life, I wouldn't. I will gladly trade the youth of 20 for the wisdom of 50 any time. I trust that I will still feel the same way about the youth of 50 when I am 70, assuming the Lord allows me to stay around that long.

What I would like to do in the next three chapters is outline some simple financial goals and strategies for the seasons of our lives. Obviously no one will fit into all the seasons at one time. If you're older than 40 you have passed the first season. If you're between 20 and 40 you won't have reached the next season—and so on. But keep on reading. Even if you are older than 60 you may not have accomplished the goals you should have, or maybe you will be able to help your children to accomplish theirs.

The typical financial logic in our generation says that a young couple should buy a home, usually based on two incomes, open an IRA to shelter some income, and start a savings plan for the children. In addition they are told they need life insurance, disability insurance, liability insurance, and a good attorney for the divorce that about half of them will face before the seventh year of marriage (because of financial troubles). I believe that logic is faulty. There are specific goals that should be met at each phase of life, not simultaneously.

135

Let's assume that one goal is to own a home (debt-free); a second is to provide adequately for our families in the event of premature death; a third is to have enough surplus to help our children with college expenses; and a fourth is to be able to give at least 20 percent of our income to the Lord's work: all by the age of 40. There can be some lesser financial goals, but if you achieve these major goals you'll be in the 3 percent of Americans who have. From this point on I'll shift from we (general) to you (specific) since this book is for you, and I'm already in the 50-to-60 stage of life myself.

Most people at age 25 are thinking about how to buy their first home, pay off their school debts, and find the "right" job. Few are really interested in what investments have the highest rates of return with the least risk. That's both understandable and normal. So what I would like to do for this group is discuss some ideas that will pay financial dividends later by helping to save money presently. Remember that investing for the future is inversely related to spending during the present.

I would like to begin by working from the smallest to the largest purchases. Attention to the smallest financial details is good training for managing larger amounts of money later.

INSURANCE

We all need some insurance in our modern society, even if it is just liability insurance for our cars or homes. The better you understand exactly what you need, the better decisions you can make. Each dollar not spent on unnecessary insurance is a dollar that can be saved toward long-term goals such as education, retirement, and elimination of debt.

Deductibles

The higher deductibles you can afford the more you will save on any type of insurance. For instance, if you elect to carry collision insurance on your car the difference between a $100 deductible or a $500 deductible can be as much as half the annual premium. Therefore, if you can absorb the first $500 in repairs you can save $150 a year or more. The key is to buy only what you need, and not be coerced into a more expensive plan than absolutely necessary. The same can be said for deductibles on home insurance, health insurance, and the like.

Combining Policies

Most people don't realize that by consolidating their insurance they can save a considerable amount of money. One company may offer a better rate on car insurance; another may have a better rate on home insurance. But usually one company will write all of your personal property insurance for less than the total of several companies. Also, if you place your property insurance with one company often they will underwrite an "umbrella" liability policy of a million dollars or more for a very small additional cost. You need to ask if this is an option before selecting any company. My insurance company provides me with such a policy and it costs me less than $100 a year extra. This can be an important asset as your financial base grows, especially in our litigating society. One lawsuit, justified or not, can destroy a lifetime of earnings.

I learned with my first home that it is much cheaper to buy my own insurance than to purchase it from the lender. A good homeowner's policy through a reputable company turned out to be less than half the cost of a fire insurance policy sold through the lender. Additionally, a homeowner's policy covers not only the dwelling but contents, liability, jewelry, clothes, and temporary housing.

I also learned that shopping for the best quality insurance at the best price is essential. The cost of insuring personal property will vary by 200 to 300 percent depending on the company you select—so shop. One of the best resources available is the *Consumer Reports* magazine. Each year it evaluates all types of insurance and reports on the assets and liabilities of the country's major insurers. You can normally find a copy of the issue you need at any public library.

Mortgage Insurance

Most mortgage lenders today require a mortgage insurance policy that will pay off the outstanding loan balance if a home buyer dies. The mortgage lender often sells an insurance policy that costs several times what an equivalent term life policy would cost from a major insurance company. My advice is to buy your own insurance and assign the amount necessary to pay off the mortgage to the lender. The savings can be significant.

Life Insurance

I can remember being approached by insurance salesmen while in college. They tried to convince (scare) me that if I didn't buy right then I might never be insurable again. The truth is only a small fraction of the population is uninsurable, and most are uninsurable from birth because of diabetes, heart abnormality, or some other congenital disease.

Later I learned that the policies many of these agents offered were inferior, overpriced, and usually blatantly deceptive. Often they were high-cost policies that were heavily financed in the front end to make them appear cheaper. Later the costs rose significantly while the protection declined. In short, they were a rip-off.

Life insurance should be used only to provide for those who are dependent on you while you are living. Otherwise it is a waste of money, in my opinion. If you are not married, or have no children, you rarely need life insurance, except for burial expenses. And if you join a memorial society, they will provide burial services at less than the cost of one year's insurance premium (in most cases).

Below the age of 40 it has been my observation that the majority of people who need life insurance are better served with "term" insurance. This is life insurance that accumulates no cash values, pays little or no dividends, and costs a fraction of what a whole life, or cash value, policy costs at the same age. The vast majority of young couples are underinsured and overextended because someone sold them a policy that was too expensive for their needs. A good, annual renewable (to age 100) insurance policy at age 25 to 35 will cost less than one tenth of an equivalent cash value policy at the same age.

If you are disciplined about following the rest of the strategy outlined in this book, your need for life insurance will diminish greatly before the term plan ever reaches the average cost of a typical cash value plan.

A young couple in their twenties can save an average of $15,000 in premiums before the age of 40 by buying term rather than cash value (whole life) insurance. That money, if invested wisely, will grow to nearly $200,000 by age 65. If you are unable to save the premium discounts between the ages of 20 and 40, your insurance strategy will need some change in the next stage of life.

Disability Insurance

Disability insurance, outside of a group plan, is generally very expensive if it is designed to provide for a loss of income for life. The cost is greatly reduced if the length of coverage is reduced. Most younger people would be better off with a plan that provides for three to five years, instead of life. Remember also that Social Security does provide for disability benefits, as does workman's compensation, if the disability is job-related.

Weighing the benefits of disability insurance is critical since the costs are high. Actual costs can vary by 50 percent or more, depending on the company. If funds are limited, disability insurance should be fairly low on your list of priorities. Again, don't be panicked by horror stories of those who failed to carry a disability policy and were permanently disabled. They are the exception to the rule. I would also add that God can still provide, regardless of anyone's disabilities. I always reflect on Joni Eareckson Tada, a guadriplegic, as an example that anyone can learn to earn a living, regardless of physical handicaps.

CREDIT CARDS

Obviously my advice is don't finance any purchases on your credit cards. The rates are usurious, and the temptation to buy things you don't need and can't afford is amplified by the easy use of credit. If you can't afford to pay cash for consumer items such as food, clothing, vacations, gas, and auto repairs, then do without them. There is no alternative if you ever expect to be financially free. I would refer you to my book, *Debt-Free Living* (Moody Press, 1989) for a complete plan on getting and staying out of debt.

AUTOMOBILES

It is usually common for most young couples to finance their first car. Unfortunately, many, if not most, opt to buy a car too expensive for their budget and plunge themselves into debt. Pick a car that fits your budget and don't be swayed by advertising that promotes cheap financing. There is no free lunch, and if a company lowers the interest rates to entice you to buy its new car, it's because the car is overpriced.

The least expensive way to finance a car commercially, especially a used car, is often through a credit union. If you are a member of a credit union, explore this alternative first. If you are not, then look for a car that can be totally paid off in two years or less and shop for a simple-interest loan. Stay away from add-on interest loans because they carry a front-end interest penalty if you want to accelerate the payments.

It is usually best not to finance a car loan through a dealer. When you mix trade-ins, finance charges, credit insurance, and sometimes even life insurance, into the deal, it's difficult to tell what the car actually costs. If you have to finance a car, arrange the loan outside and negotiate with the dealer as if you were paying cash—which you are. The convenience of dealer financing is often very costly.

I believe that Christian parents should help their children

with their first home and car, if they can afford to do so. Sometimes it is just a matter of asking parents who have the means if they will help. Just be certain that you treat any family loan with the same respect and discipline you would a bank loan. If the parents want to discount the loan, that is their right, not the borrower's.

HOME LOANS

One of the best ways to finance a home is by borrowing the funds from a pension or retirement plan. It is possible for anyone to extend a first mortgage loan from their retirement account to a nondependent. I personally know many Christians who have done so to help young couples get into their first homes. The obvious advantage is that there are no discount points, closing costs are minimal, and the loan is backed by the home so the retirement account is protected. Typically the loan is arranged at whatever the prevailing government T-bill rate is, usually 2 to 3 percent less than a commercial loan.

Most home loans today are for 30 years, but just paying an extra $100 a month will retire a $100,000 loan approximately 12 years early and save nearly $140,000 in interest charges that can be used to start a long-term investment program, as mentioned earlier.

A second option is owner financing. This is where the person selling the home becomes the lender. Obviously the home must be debt-free for the owner to be able to do this. This is often the best arrangement for both parties. The buyer can arrange a lower interest rate and avoid the discount point penalties normally required by a commercial lender. The seller benefits through the up-front down payment, the home is collateral for the loan, and the interest rate is higher than the prevailing rates they could earn through a bank deposit.

If financing cannot be arranged through a retirement account or owner financing, shop for the best rate available. Often financing for a shorter period, such as 15 years, can save 1 percent or more in annual interest. On a $100,000 mortgage, 1 percent interest saved amounts to $1,000 the first year.

There are often government programs available for first-time home buyers at preferred interest rates. Since the programs change frequently, you will have to verify them as the need arises.

INVESTMENT GOALS

It is my strong conviction that becoming debt-free, including the home mortgage, should be the first investment goal for any young couple (or person). Once you have achieved that goal, then, and only then, should you invest in other areas. As I said earlier, the exception to this would be a company retirement account with matching company funds where the proceeds could be withdrawn at some future date to retire a home mortgage.

Let's assume that by the age of 35 you have achieved the goal of becoming debt-free and want to move to the next step, the accumulation of education funds. If the children are within five years of college, at least half of all available funds should be kept in investments that can easily be converted into cash as needed. Normally these will be no-load mutual funds, short-term bonds, or liquid savings plans such as money market funds and CDs.

As the children begin college the investment plan can be temporarily curtailed so that current funds can be used for many of the annual expenses. This is really a matter of matching your available funds and costs. The use of local community colleges or state schools can stretch available funds significantly.

Assuming that you have enough surplus funds to meet the need for college, these funds should be accumulated in relatively low-risk investments. Again the prevailing principle is that no greater risks should be assumed than are necessary to meet your goals.

If the funds are insufficient, then higher risks must be assumed. Under any circumstances, the maximum risks that should be taken with designated college funds are probably good quality growth mutual funds. If you can accumulate only enough funds to help your children attend a local community college, that is better than to risk everything and not be able to send them at all.

SYSTEMATIC SAVINGS

Perhaps the single most important part of any investment strategy between the ages of 20 and 40 is systematic and regular savings. The temptation, once the home is paid off, is to increase your spending level because the additional funds are available. Most young couples with potential surpluses consume it on bigger houses, cars, boats, motor homes, and vacations. Controlling these indulgences must be a part of your long-term plans.

For instance, if you have a two- or three-step plan to move up in housing, stick to it. After the third move into the home you have agreed will meet your needs, resist the temptation to move up again. Often to do so will delay your getting debt-free well into your fifties, if ever.

As I said earlier, I prefer mutual funds as a savings vehicle for most people because they will normally accept monthly payments of as little as $10, or as much as you can afford.

Obviously, a reasonable cash reserve should be maintained for emergencies such as layoffs, illnesses, additional children, and emergency giving. The normal formula for emergency savings is approximately three months of income, although this will vary according to your profession. A postal worker has less need for a large cash reserve than does a real estate agent by virtue of their respective professions.

If by the age of 40 you have your home debt-free, have saved at least one half of your first two children's college education expenses, and have begun a long-term investment plan, you will have accomplished more than 95 percent of all Americans today. You're ready to move on to phase two.

12

The Financial Seasons of Life:
Ages 40 to 60

I f, at age 40, you have achieved the goals outlined in the previous chapter, you are ready to ascend to the next stage of your financial life. But if you have not been able to become debt-free, including your home, you need to make that your priority. One bit of counsel I would offer is, don't panic or start speculating wildly as a substitute for good, sound planning, even if you're approaching your sixties. God is still able to provide what is needed. Rethink your strategy to accomplish the debt-free goals in this phase and adjust your retirement goals to later in life.

For those who are now facing children's college expenses but have no surpluses to cover them, I would offer some additional counsel: Don't plunge further into debt to send your children to college by taking out a home equity loan, government loan, or the like. Help your children to the extent that you can without taking on more debt. They will need to adjust to attending a local junior or community college, and working their way through college to a large extent. Prior to the easy credit years of the seventies and eighties, that's how most of us made it through college. Let me assure you that it can still be done, and your kids will survive, in spite of their wailing to the contrary. This can be an opportunity for them (and you) to trust the Lord in a visible and objective way. God can still provide for our needs, including the education of our children, despite all the ways we have found to circumvent it.

Some time back I was talking with a long-time friend who was suffering some financial setbacks. He was lamenting the fact that his daughter was being forced to leave the university she had been attending for three years because he was not able to secure a loan to help her financially. When he paused, I responded, "Well, praise the Lord for that."

Unfortunately he didn't see it that way and took offense. He informed me that his daughter was a member of the honor club, the college drama club, the glee club, and several other activities. "For her to leave college would cause her to miss out on one of life's great opportunities," he told me irritatedly.

I assured him that I was not playing the role of one of Job's friends, proclaiming that he was being punished by God. I explained what I believe the Scripture says: to borrow more money (for any reason) when you cannot repay what you have already borrowed is contrary to God's will. As Proverbs 3:28 says, "Do not say to your neighbor, 'Go, and come back, and tomorrow I will give it,' when you have it with you." When you borrow while in debt you risk the existing creditors' positions. Literally you rob them of assets they are owed.

My friend didn't really want to hear anything further, so for the next 30 minutes we ate breakfast in relative silence. It was several weeks before I heard from him again. He called to tell me that his daughter was attending a local college in their city, and loving it. She had been trying to find a way to tell her parents that she did not want to go back to the university she had been attending. The drinking, sex, profanity, and open use of drugs at the school ran contrary to everything she had been taught to believe. She had stuck it out for two years only because she felt that to quit would have let her parents down. She has now graduated from college, is working part-time for a Christian state senator, and is looking forward to attending law school on a full grant-in-aid from a local law firm that wants her on their team when she graduates. Sometimes it is necessary for us to step back and allow God to do His will.

FORTY AND AGING

By the age of 40 if you have not settled into a lifestyle you sincerely believe is God's plan for your family, you need to do so. Too often these become the indulgent years when couples buy airplanes, motor homes, large boats, second homes, or sports cars. Within reason, some additional spending is possible once education needs are met. But there will never be enough surplus to buy all the grown-up toys that are available today.

There are two general lifestyle strategies I have observed in the 40-to-60 age group. Obviously there are always exceptions to the rule; but these aren't rules, they're observations.

One strategy is for a couple to maximize their living standard by buying the home they always wanted but could never afford while the kids were at home. This strategy means that the majority of their available assets will be sunk in a home, and perhaps a vacation condo. This allows the kids to come back with the grandchildren at holidays and vacations. It also means (for most people) another lifestyle change at retirement. I am not speaking about those who make $100,000 a year or more during this 20-year period. Their choices are broader and often they can have the home they desire and still invest in other assets for retirement. This is not meant to be an indictment or an approval, simply an observation.

If you establish this strategy, then the sale of the home just before retirement is critical because so much of your net worth is invested in it. Such a lifestyle change can be traumatic and, in truth, many couples won't make that decision until they realize that taxes, utilities, maintenance, and insurance consume too much of their income after retirement. Sometimes they are forced to sell their home in a down market and lose a large part of their net worth.

If the majority of your net worth is in your home, you need to be realistic about when (or if) you can retire. If you are forced to retire by company policy you will need to adopt a budget matching your retirement income at least five years early (by age 60) to assess whether or not the home fits your budget. If not, allow enough time to sell it at market value.

The second strategy used by those 40 to 60, planning toward retirement at 65, is to pare down, move into a smaller home, and free more money for investing and traveling during these years. Some friends of ours recently made this move—to the dismay of their children, who didn't want their parents to sell the home they had lived in for more than 20 years. But our friends decided they would take advantage of the one-time capital gains exclusion of $125,000 on their residence, buy a smaller home, and invest the difference.

They also wanted to do some traveling during these years without constantly being tied down to a home that required a great deal of maintenance and upkeep. They purchased a much smaller home on sale from the Resolution Trust Corporation (selling defunct S&L assets) for about $50,000 in cash, bought a summer cottage in the mountains of North Carolina for $40,000, and still had well over $100,000 to invest for retirement. Their overall housing expenses dropped from about $600 a month for utilities, maintenance, and taxes to about $250.

They obviously had to make some sacrifices in terms of lifestyle. Their children could no longer all gather at one time in their parents' home. So now they all go to one of the other children's homes for Christmas, birthdays, and other special occasions. The children can still visit their parents' home, but only one family at a time since they have only one free bedroom and a small study available. Obviously this is a strategy that affects everyone in the family and requires a lot of prayer, but this couple, and many others, believe it will pay financial dividends in the long run.

INSURANCE NEEDS

Those in the 40-to-60 age range will quickly discover that the term insurance they bought earlier, at a very low rate, gets progressively more expensive the longer they live. By the age of 50, term insurance begins to get prohibitively expensive, unless the insured is very healthy and can qualify for a reduced rate.

The alternatives available for life insurance narrow down rapidly after age 50. Basically, you can continue to pay the high cost of term (if you can afford it); you can reduce the face value of your policy, thereby reducing the premium; or you can convert the term to whole life (assuming your policy provides that option).

For me, the best option was to reduce my coverage, which reduced my annual costs. That option was available because my need for life insurance had declined. In my case it was because we had our home paid for, our children grown, and were saving some of our earnings regularly. I still needed *some* life insurance in the event that I died before my wife reached 62 and until our investments matured to provide for her income.

Often insurance agents make the argument that life insurance can be used to pay estate taxes, which is true. But since the estate tax laws were changed to allow a surviving spouse to receive unlimited assets, that argument isn't economically logical, in my opinion. The money you leave your children or grandchildren is surplus, not necessity, unless they are totally dependent on you. It doesn't make a lot of economic sense to me to pay an insurance company a profit to leave children something they don't really need anyway. But you may feel differently, which is your right.

I converted a term life insurance policy with a face value of $150,000 to a modified whole life policy at age 49. I did so primarily because of the need for at least that amount for my wife, who was then 46. I selected an option, called a split-dollar plan, that allows the premiums to be paid in lieu of salary and then I pay the income taxes due. There are a thousand ways to arrange life insurance. If you'll find a good independent agent, I'll guarantee that he'll find a way to sell you what you need at a price you can afford.

RISK

The 40-to-60 age period is when you should logically be able to absorb the highest degree of risk. If you're debt-free, have your children's college expenses taken care of, and can afford to take some risk with a portion of your surplus, now's the time. Just make the absolute rule—*no surety!* With no surety the worst that can happen is you lose the money you have at risk. Obviously I'm not suggesting taking foolish risks. But in these years you can look for investments that multiply, as opposed to simply earning interest. The exceptions to this strategy are investors who can earn all the money they will ever need, in which case, as I said before, why take the risk?

Other exceptions are widows, divorcees, disabled people, etc. Remember that risk is not just a factor of age. It relates to temperament, income, and ability to replace the funds that can be lost. For instance, a widow in her early forties with a lump sum from her husband's estate to invest, probably needs to adopt the "60-plus" strategy. She should be primarily concerned with preservation of capital, not growth. I realize that this is repetitive, but it cannot be stressed enough—do not assume a risk above what you can afford to lose, regardless of your age!

USE OF RETIREMENT ACCOUNTS

If you have access to a retirement account, it is normally a good way to invest for the long term. As I said earlier, there are exceptions. I personally would not invest in a company retirement account where my investment choices were controlled by others and the past track record was poor. I would rather pay the taxes and earn 10 percent on the remainder than invest tax-deferred income in a plan that has lost half of the money entrusted to it.

IRAs are the most flexible retirement accounts available to average-income investors and should be a high priority for those who can qualify to use them. It has been my observation that many people do not understand that IRAs are *not* investments themselves. They are retirement *accounts* that shelter income by deferring the income taxes until the funds are withdrawn. An IRA can contain any type of investment that is available to the general public. For instance, an IRA can contain mutual funds, stocks, bonds, CDs, Treasury bills, and so on. You can also establish IRAs that are "self-directed," meaning that you place the money in a cash account such as a money market fund, then later direct the administrator where you want the money invested. (NOTE: Self-directed IRAs are usually available through selected banks. Most banks charge an annual administration fee that ranges from $10 to $50. Check with your bank about their fees and policies before establishing a self-directed IRA.)

You can also cancel one IRA and transfer the funds into another IRA, provided you do so within the prescribed time frame (presently 60 days), without additional tax consequences. At present such transfers are limited to one a year.

Self-employed people, and those who work for them, have access to several good retirement plans (at the time of this writing) including an HR-10 (Keogh) plan, a Self-Employed Pension plan (SEP), and IRAs. Since a portion of my income is generated from book royalties and constitutes self-employment income, I can shelter a portion of my earning in an SEP each year, even though I also have a portion of my income earned as an employee of a nonprofit organization.

The SEP is flexible and is offered by virtually all investment companies as an option. The funds are invested according to your personal choices and can be transferred if necessary. For instance, I purchased a variable annuity several years back that projected a 9 percent return on investment. Instead it averaged only 6 percent after all administrative charges. So I withdrew the funds from the annuity and reinvested them in a mutual fund. The mutual fund company provided all the forms and handled the transaction at no cost to me. They also provided an 800-number service to answer any questions I might have. The same procedure can be used to transfer funds from an IRA, HR-10, or company plan to any other qualified retirement account.

It is important to note that although the current law restricts any one individual's annual contribution to an IRA to no more than $2,000, that rule does not apply to transfers from another qualified retirement account. So you could have $25,000 in an HR-10 or SEP and still transfer the proceeds into an IRA without incurring a penalty.

The bottom line is, if you can use a tax-deferred retirement plan without sacrificing good investment strategy, do so. A list of the various plans that exist as of this writing are listed in the Appendix.

PLANS AND GOALS

Before developing a plan it is necessary first to define your goals. Your goal may be to retire with 80 percent of your present income at age 62. Someone else may desire to retire on 50 percent of his (or her) income at age 59 and supplement income from another source. Still others may want to continue to work for as long as possible, while storing some reserve in the event they are unable to work at a later time. Whatever your goals, they should be well defined and compatible with God's plan for your life. There is no easy answer to some of these questions. They require a great deal of prayer and communication between spouses.

Let's assume that your goal (at age 40) is to retire at age 62 on at least 70 percent of your present income ($40,000 a year) and work for a nonprofit organization 20 hours a week earning at least an additional 10 percent of your salary. Based on current Social Security benefits, you could expect to receive approximately $15,000 a year in retirement benefits.

That means in 22 years you need to have saved at least $150,000 that could then be invested conservatively to earn $14,000 a year.

Let's also assume that you can realistically save $3,000 a year between now and 62 for a total contribution of $66,000 ($3,000 x 22). You can accomplish your goals easily by investing in one or more good quality mutual funds that average approximately 8 percent real growth a year. The choices for this level of return are plentiful.

For instance, had you invested in one of the 10 leading mutual funds over the last 20 years, your investment of $66,000 would have grown to nearly $200,000. Obviously, nothing guarantees that any investment plan will match past performance; but if you follow the strategy I outlined earlier and switch funds if necessary, you should be able to achieve the needed return.

Remember that the concept of goal-setting is critical and deceptively simple. You need to know what you are trying to accomplish and then select the investments that will achieve those goals with the least risk possible.

I'll use one more example before moving on to the next stage. Let's assume that at age 50 you succeed in becoming debt-free. Now you have $400 a month to invest (after taxes) and your goal is to retire at age 65 on at least 75 percent of your current income of $30,000 a year.

Social Security retirement benefits will be approximately $12,000 per year. Your monthly saving will total $72,000 ($400 x 12 = $4,800 annually x 15 years) at age 65. Your income needs above Social Security would be $10,500 a year. In order to provide that amount from your retirement account it will have to grow to at least $150,000 by age 65.

If you had the entire $72,000 to invest at age 50 that would be no problem. At 8 percent interest your money would double every nine years. Even after taxes it would grow to the needed amount by retirement. But you don't have the entire amount to invest; it's being accumulated incrementally at the rate of $400 a month. So your earnings on the money will need to average about 15 percent a year to meet your goal.

Several investments have earned this amount over the last decade. However, again it is important to note that all earnings are based on past history (since that is all the history we have to go on). You cannot park your money in one or more of these investments and forget it. You will need to watch them and move the funds if necessary. Any investment that averages less than the needed 15 percent over any five-year period would need to be changed.

I would personally use good quality mutual funds to accomplish this goal also, since it is well within the range of growth funds, particularly those specializing in international stocks. These funds have performed well in spite of economic slowdowns in any single country. Funds like Vanguard and Twentieth Century International have averaged nearly 20 percent a year growth over the last 10 years. Hopefully they will in the future. If not, then trade for those that do.

The strategy for those in the 40-to-60 age range is to come out of this stage of life debt-free, goals clearly in mind, and the majority of the needed funds in well-performing investments.

It really doesn't matter whether you select mutual funds, stocks, annuities, real estate, or antique cars, as long as you are on track with your goals. The more funds you have available, the more you can and should diversify. Just keep in mind that once you have met your goals anything else saved is hoarding, not saving. Pray about your goals (husband and wife together). Then stick to them. If inflation, taxes, or your investments change drastically, be ready to make adjustments. Remember that God doesn't hold us accountable for things we cannot control, only for those we can.

13

The Financial Seasons of Life:
Age 60 and Up

From age 60 on, an investor who has achieved the goals from the previous two stages of life will enter the "preservation" mode. Basically this means that you, the investor, need to concentrate on preserving what you have worked so hard to accumulate.

Obviously if you have not achieved the goals set in the previous stages, you will need to delay your retirement plans and work to become debt-free, accumulate the supplemental funds you and your spouse will need, and adopt a very conservative lifestyle. It is unfortunate that so few Americans establish any realistic financial goals early in life and face the 60-plus years with unrealistic expectations.

The most common mistake most Americans make is to retire without adequate financial preparation. They simply believe that 62 or 65 represents the "mandatory" retirement age, regardless of their situation. Two points need to be made here: First, there is no mandatory retirement age (not biblically). Many people can and do remain gainfully employed long into their seventies and even eighties. Perhaps they cannot work as hard, but they have learned to work a lot smarter.

Second, you cannot take a 50-percent (or more) cut in income and expect to enjoy your retirement years. Unless you have adjusted to the projected retirement income level at least three years prior to retirement, you're fooling yourself.

Often those who retire without adequate preparation find themselves trying to reenter the job market shortly after retiring only to find that they can't earn anywhere near the salary level they left. Many end up taking entry-level jobs at very low wages. They would have been far better off to have stayed at the job they left. Current laws prohibit mandatory retirement, except in age critical professions, such as airline pilot. So retirement is an option, not a requirement.

Let me restate an absolute. If you can't adjust to the projected income you expect to receive after retirement at least three years before that time—stay where you are! Reset your retirement goals to 65, 68, or 80, but don't become a poverty statistic. As Christ said in Luke 14:28-30:

> For which one of you, when he wants to build a tower, does not first sit down and calculate the cost, to see if he has enough to complete it? Otherwise, when he has laid a foundation, and is not able to finish, all who observe it begin to ridicule him, saying, "This man began to build and was not able to finish."

I saw an interesting example of this principle at work a few years back. Phil and Andy, both in their sixties, worked for a wholesale automobile supply company. Andy, the delivery man (called an expeditor), earned about $12,000 a year. Phil, the plant manager, earned about $40,000 a year. Neither had put any significant savings aside, nor had either taken advantage of the company's retirement plan. Phil, the plant manager, obviously lived in a bigger home and drove better cars, and took better vacations during his working career.

At age 62 each elected to take an early retirement option from the company. Andy received a lump sum of about $10,000 from the company; Phil received a lump sum of about $35,000.

By coincidence both men came in for counseling about two years after retirement. Andy had adjusted very well to his Social Security income, in addition to working a part-time delivery job that paid him about $50 a week. In fact, Andy and his wife were actually better off financially than when he had been fully employed. All they needed was some budgeting help to maintain better control of some nonmonthly expenses such as annual insurance, home taxes, and car repairs.

Phil, on the other hand, was in deep financial trouble. He had spent all of his severance bonus and had run up sizable credit card debts. The reason was obvious. He had taken more than a 50-percent cut in income to retire on Social Security alone. The severance bonus buffered him for a little more than a year, but when it ran out his lifestyle crashed in on him. Phil attempted to find work also but could locate only minimum wage jobs.

In reality Andy, the delivery man, was better prepared than his boss. He made nearly a lateral move into retirement because he never had the money to indulge or to accumulate any debt to speak of. Phil took a drastic income reduction and was unable to make the adjustment. The principle is taught clearly in Proverbs 12:9, "Better is he who is lightly esteemed and has a servant, than he who honors himself and lacks bread."

ALTERNATE INCOME

Before discussing financial strategy for those 60 and older I would like to share an observation: A marketable skill is the most dependable retirement plan anyone can have. As long as you are reasonably healthy, you will never be listed among the impoverished in our society.

This idea is neither new nor original with me. It is a concept that was traditional until the last two generations. Most young men learned a trade while they were at home. Even if they left that trade and went to college or into another business, the skill was still retained. I used this approach to work my way through college long before any banker was crazy enough to lend a college student money.

When I was in high school I knew that my family would not

be able financially to help me go to college. So for several summers in high school I worked as an apprentice electrician and attended night classes twice a week to pass the journeyman electrician's license test. By the time I finished high school I had my license and was earning about $3 an hour, while my friends who worked in grocery stores or retail stores were making $1.25 an hour. That trade allowed me to work my way through college at the Cape Canaveral Space Center in Florida, eventually becoming a manager of an experiments station. Although I have not worked at the trade for nearly 25 years now, I still remember the fundamentals and could market that skill to earn a living if necessary. Anyone approaching retirement who has doubts about having enough income can do the same thing. Just sign up for night classes at any good vocational school and learn a trade that suits your abilities; you'll always have an income. If you don't believe it, just try to hire someone to check out your air conditioner (or fix a faucet, or build a closet, or paint your house) and see what it costs.

RETIREMENT STRATEGY

For those who have met the required criteria for 60-plus— they are debt-free and have enough investment savings for the winter years—it's time to start making some adjustments in strategy. The basic strategy for over 60 is to develop a more conservative long-range outlook. The principal objective now becomes one of protection and conservation, rather than growth.

That does not mean to shift all of your assets into U.S. Treasury bills. Your strategy may be as simple as shifting from high-growth mutual funds to income funds. Usually any mutual fund company offers a wide range of investment pools or mixes, each with a differing objective. By requesting a prospectus, any investor can determine which of the plans best fits the age and strategy needed.

I have chosen to use a tiered system to describe the types of investments used at each stage of life. You will notice a decided shift toward the conservative end of the tier at this point. It doesn't matter whether you elect to use mutual funds, stocks, real estate, or collectibles to build your investment base; you still need to shift strategies with enough of your assets to secure the income you need to live on.

By adopting this more conservative strategy, you will probably miss out on some of the major stock market rallies, as well as some of the better "deals" offered by your brother-in-law who just went to work for the plasma engine dealer. Such is life. If you want to retire with some degree of financial security you will need to make such sacrifices. The whole object from age 60 on is to try to avoid the disasters that can wipe you out totally.

If, after securing the major portion of your assets, you still have funds with which to speculate, that is a decision between you, your spouse, and the Lord.

Remember that the one variable in this age-related strategy is inflation. If inflation is re-ignited by the massive debt spending of our government, you will need to adjust your planning. Inflation can erode your long-term assets just as surely as a bad investment can.

THE TIERED SHIFT

Let's assume that you are approaching 60-plus and have achieved most of your goals through the use of mutual funds and rental real estate. Now you need to make the necessary adjustments to a more conservative posture. The following illustration shows how your funds could have been allocated up to this point. The majority (nearly 80 percent) of the investments were oriented toward some aggressive funds during your forties and fifties. The only funds left in the most conservative tier were those used to pay for college educations as they came due.

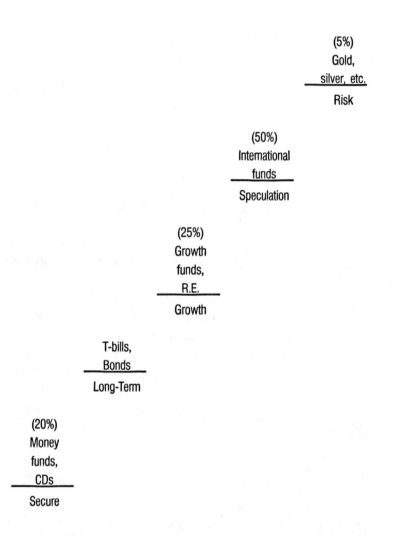

(5%)
Gold,
silver, etc.
Risk

(50%)
International
funds
Speculation

(25%)
Growth
funds,
R.E.
Growth

T-bills,
Bonds
Long-Term

(20%)
Money
funds,
CDs
Secure

Now the shift to the conservative side is necessary. About six months' salary will be maintained in a cash reserve account to meet emergencies. As the regular dividend income is received, it is deposited in this account. Once the account accumulates more than eight months' reserve, it is shifted to a longer term cash reserve account, such as a CD, to earn more interest.

The goal is to maintain a spendable income of approximately $2,500 per month at retirement—including Social Security, investment earnings, and some generated income.

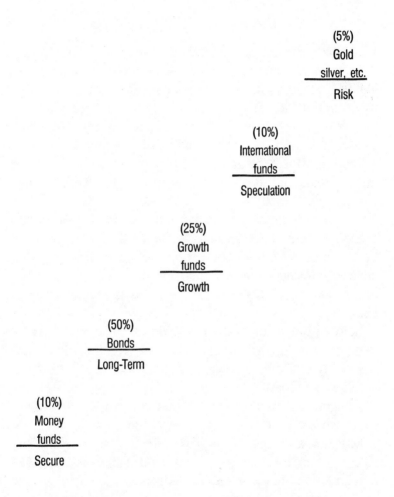

(5%)
Gold
silver, etc.
Risk

(10%)
International
funds
Speculation

(25%)
Growth
funds
Growth

(50%)
Bonds
Long-Term

(10%)
Money
funds
Secure

One additional note here: Since earned income can affect your Social Security pension, it is critical to shift as much of the earned income as possible to unearned income. There are several ways to do this. It should be noted that the tax laws change frequently so these options may or may not be available at the time of your retirement. However, the one certainty is that some options will always be available since our elected officials also retire.

USING A CORPORATION

If you have earned income and can shelter it within a corporate structure, you can avoid some of the earned-income liability. The corporation can provide medical, life, and disability insurance without affecting your Social Security income. It can also retain the earnings or profits and redistribute them as dividends. Obviously, there would be some additional tax considerations. But if the amount of corporate income taxes paid are less than the loss of Social Security due to earned income, you will still benefit.

Also a corporation can offer you a Section 125 plan (often called a Cafeteria Plan) where 100 percent of your salary can be assigned. From this plan you can pay all medical expenses, child care for dependents, dental, eye care, etc. This does not affect your Social Security earnings and is exempt from all taxes.

Before using a corporation to shelter income, it is essential that you consult a good tax accountant. Tax laws do change frequently and only a working professional in the field can advise you properly.

I will use the example of a Christian I'll call Don to demonstrate what can be done with some good planning.

Don was a computer specialist with a large company and elected to accept their early retirement plan at age 62, even though he had not planned to leave the company for several more years. The early retirement package, including a lump-sum settlement, actually provided him with more than the amount he would have earned during the following five years, had he continued to work.

Don had a specific retirement goal: He desired to do volunteer mission work with his church six months of the year and operate a computer consulting company the other six months.

He invested the majority of the lump-sum settlement in conservative bonds and other securities. This provided him with a monthly income of approximately $2,000. In addition, his Social Security provided another $1,200 per month. This amount would have been higher except that Don had been exempt from the system for 10 years earlier in his life.

Don and his wife lived in an extremely high-cost area of the country and desired to remain there as long as possible to work with their church and stay close to their children and grandchildren. In order to do so, Don required an additional $600 per month. So he established a corporation through which he would do his consulting. The company provided him with a supplemental health care plan for Medicare, a company vehicle, and a Section 125 plan to pay for all additional health-related expenses, thus dropping his total monthly expenses by nearly $400. Once a year Don would also receive a dividend check from the company, providing the remaining income he required (on which he had to pay income taxes). Since the dividend was not earned income, his Social Security benefits were not affected.

As the company accumulated retained earnings, Don used some of the funds for the ministry he was involved in, as well as for a cash reserve in times of emergency.

In a matter of months Don had shifted his strategy from a retirement age of 67 to 62 with no reduction in annual income. By January of the next year he and his wife were doing mission work in Central America, helping to evangelize business people in that area—a goal he had established as a part of his strategy nearly 10 years earlier.

CATCHING THE VISION

I trust that by now you have correctly assessed the rationale behind planning for the stages of life. It is to allow you to shift your priorities as you mature.

The first priority of any Christian is to serve the Lord with all of his heart, soul, and mind (Matthew 22:37). To do that effectively requires some ordering of priorities. The beginning stage should be to free ourselves from debt so that our families are secure financially, regardless of what happens in our economy. The second stage is to accumulate a surplus to meet ordinary expenses, such as education, and to set aside some surplus for later. The third stage is to free ourselves to continue to be active and serve others without the pressures of earning and accumulating the needed funds through daily labor.

Retirement therefore is not what most Americans think of as the time to stop all gainful employment. Rather it is the time to shift into a higher gear, free from the pressures of the competitive work world to a large degree. If, for some reason, the Lord allows the entire U.S. economy to fail, including many of our own investments, we will have the assurance of knowing that we were the best possible stewards of the resources He gave us to manage. The worst that can happen to us is to lose some or all of our surpluses and continue to work at whatever level we are capable. Being debt-free makes that strategy a lot more feasible.

One closing thought on the concept of staying active: Several recent studies have shown that many men and women once thought to suffer from irreversible senility recovered much of their earlier abilities by daily exposure to mental and physical stimulation. Some studies even indicated that active older people experience a regeneration of brain activity, once thought to be impossible. It is not surprising that the scientific community is beginning to discover what we Christians already knew: God created us to be productive beings throughout our *entire* lifespan. As the old cliché goes: "Use it or lose it."

14

Evaluating Investments:
The Five-Tier System

I would like to present briefly some of the more common investments available and place them on what I referred to in the previous chapter as the "tiered" system (tiered according to how I rate them for risk and return). I trust this will help you later as you consider which investments are right for your plan. (NOTE: This is an expansion of material I have previously covered in my book *The Complete Financial Guide for Young Couples.*)

I have simply assigned a scale from 0 to 10 that can be applied to each type of investment. Zero represents the least return or the least risk, and 10 represents the highest risk or highest return. Therefore, an investment with an income potential of 0 and a risk factor of 10 would represent the worst possible investment. An investment with an income potential of 10 and a risk of 0 would be the best investment. You can't find those, by the way.

I have also added a third factor: growth. Growth means the ability of an investment to appreciate, such as common stocks. Investments such as bonds have a potential growth factor also. If a bond pays a yield of 10 percent and interest rates drop to 8 percent, the bond value increases, and vice versa.

The investments will be divided into the five basic tiers:

Tier 1. *Secure Income:* Selected because it generates cash with very little risk.

Tier 2. *Long-Term:* Selected for stability of earnings for one-year deposits or longer.

Tier 3. *Growth Investments:* Selected primarily for long-term appreciation.

Tier 4. *Speculative:* A mix between growth and speculation.

Tier 5. *High-Risk:* Selected for their volatility and maximum growth potential.

Remember that the rating for each type of investment is purely my evaluation. It should not be accepted as an absolute. Times and economic conditions constantly change, and the degree of return or risk for most types of investments will change with the economy. When interest rates and inflation are high, real property, residential housing, apartment complexes, or office buildings generally do well. But when interest rates and inflation are down, stocks and bonds generally do well.

TIER 1:
SECURE INCOME INVESTMENTS

Government Securities (Income 5)(Growth 0)(Risk 1)
Treasury bills (T-bills), Government National Mortgage Association bonds (Ginnie Mae), and savings bonds all fall into this category.

Bank Securities (Income 5)(Growth 0)(Risk 3-4)
One advantage of bank investments like savings accounts, certificates of deposit (CDs), and insured money funds is that you can invest with smaller amounts of money. It generally takes $10,000 to $25,000 to purchase a Treasury bill, but you can purchase a CD for as little as $500. The disadvantages are that they offer little or no growth because the payout is fixed and the income is taxable as it is earned.

Be certain that you invest with a bank or savings and loan protected by the FDIC or a credit union insured up to $100,000. If worse comes to worst, the government will print the money to pay what it owes. If you elect to tie up your money long-term and have a choice between a government security or bank note, I recommend the government security, because it is a primary obligation of the government.

TIER 2:
LONG-TERM INCOME INVESTMENTS

Municipal Bonds (Income 5)(Growth 0)(Risk 7-8)
These are bonds issued by a local municipality, usually a larger city such as Houston or Hartford. The primary selling feature is that most or all of the income from municipal bonds is exempt from federal income tax (and state income tax in the state where they are issued).

The liabilities of municipal bonds are: (1) they have low yields; (2) they normally require a large initial investment; and (3) they are illiquid, meaning that if you have to sell them, you will normally do so at a loss. With the exception of buying some municipal bonds for diversification, most average investors are better off with government bonds.

Take for example an investor in a 15-percent federal and 3-percent state tax bracket. A $10,000 municipal bond paying 5 percent interest yields $500. A CD paying 9 percent would yield $738 after taxes. The yield on the CD is better and the risk is less.

Mortgages (Income 8)(Growth 0-5)(Risk 3-4)
A mortgage is a contract to lend someone money to buy a home or other real property. The lender (investor) holds the mortgage rights to the property until the loan is totally repaid. Mortgage repurchase agreements are commonly offered by commercial lenders who want to resell loans they have made. The seller normally discounts the mortgage to yield from 1 to 3 percent above the prevailing interest rates. So if current interest rates on CDs are 7 percent, you can earn 8 to 10 percent through repurchased first mortgage loans.

The risk on this type of investment is relatively low because you have real property backing the loan. If a borrower fails to pay, you can foreclose on the property. The key here is the value of the property securing the mortgage. I suggest that any investment in a first mortgage be backed with property valued at two to three times the outstanding loan.

The liabilities of this kind of investment are: (1) they are hard to find—it's usually necessary to know a local attorney or a banker who will handle them; (2) the return on your investment is 100 percent taxable, as ordinary income; (3) there is no growth on your principal, unless interest rates drop, in which case your mortgage might be worth more; and (4) your money will be tied up for a long time, usually from 15 to 20 years.

If you're looking for long-term income, a first mortgage is a good way to invest. If you're selling property that you own debt-free, consider taking a first mortgage for the amount you were going to invest for income purposes. Often you can earn a higher rate of interest with less risk than virtually any other investment.

Second mortgages usually yield a higher return, with an equivalent higher risk. If you lend money on a second mortgage and the borrower defaults, you must assume the first mortgage (if it is in default too) as well as any outstanding property taxes in order to protect your equity. Many states do not allow foreclosure for default on second mortgage loans so, in order to collect, you must file a personal judgment suit against the borrower and have a levy attached to the property. If the property is ever sold, your levy must be paid once the first mortgage loan is satisfied.

Corporate Bonds (Income 6-8)(Growth 0-3)(Risk 5-6)
A corporate bond is a note issued by a corporation to finance its operation. Quality bonds often yield 2 to 3 percent higher interest rates than an equivalent CD or T-bill. The amount of return depends on the rating of the company issuing the bond.

Bonds are rated from a low of C to a high of AAA. The higher the grade of the bond, the lower the rate of return, but the risk is lower as well.

In this era of junk bonds and leveraged buyouts, the rating of a company can change quickly. In my opinion, most average investors would be far better off using a bond mutual fund to achieve the long-term income they seek. The returns are slightly lower, but the risks are lessened through diversification in many companies' bonds.

Many investors prefer bonds which generate current income through business operations, such as utility company bonds. In the past, public utility company bonds have been very stable and predictable. However, many utilities have suffered massive debts from nuclear power station construction, making them greater risks. In general, though, most utility bonds are safe investments.

One liability with corporate bonds is that repayment depends on the success of *one* company. If that company defaults, the assets of the entire company can be lost—including your bond money. Another negative is that the income is totally taxable. A bond has little chance for growth unless your rate of return is in excess of the current interest rates.

Insurance Annuity (Income 3-4)(Growth 0)(Risk 5-6)

This investment requires a prescribed amount of money to be paid into the annuity, and then the issuing insurance company promises a monthly income after retirement age.

The advantages of investing in annuities are: (1) the earnings are allowed to accumulate, tax deferred, until you retire; (2) the investment is fairly liquid, so if you have to get your money out, you can, although there is often a penalty; and (3) compared to other tax-sheltered investments, the returns are good.

But be aware that the stated yield of an insurance annuity isn't necessarily what you will receive. Sometimes the percentage given is a gross figure from which sales and administrative costs are deducted. It's best to ask for a net figure to do your comparisons and get all quotes in writing from the agent offering the annuity.

Stock Dividends (Income 4-5)(Growth 0-10)(Risk 6-7)

Common stocks usually pay dividends based on the earnings of the company. One advantage is that stocks can be purchased for relatively small amounts of money. It's possible to invest in a stock paying a dividend of 7 to 8 percent and invest less than $100. This obviously appeals to the small investor. Since the dividend is totally related to the success of the issuing company, I would look for a company that has paid dividends for many years, particularly during economic hard times.

Be aware, though, that just because a corporation has paid dividends for decades doesn't necessarily mean that it can continue to do so. The automobile industry in the early eighties is a good example. Some of the companies that had paid high rates of return for three and four decades had to cut their returns drastically. Most eventually recovered, but the people who depended on the dividends went through some lean times. So, if you plan to invest in stocks for income, you need to assess the degree of risk.

As stated previously, a good quality mutual fund can lessen the risk while achieving the same results. Professional management, together with broad diversification, provide a great advantage.

Money Funds (Income 4-5)(Growth 0)(Risk 2-8)

Money funds are the pooled funds of many people used to purchase short-term securities. These are not true savings accounts, but are short-term mutual funds that pay interest. Shares normally sell for $1 each but can vary, depending on the fund's assets value. Money funds are available through most brokerage firms, savings and loans, and banks; those offered by brokerage firms are not federally insured against losses. The interest rates are normally adjusted monthly.

It is extremely important to verify the rating of any money fund frequently. If the rating drops below an "A," remove your money and select another fund. Also, don't maintain more than $25,000 or 10 percent of your assets (whichever is lower) in any one money fund.

TIER 3:
GROWTH INVESTMENTS

This tier is in the middle and represents the crossover from conservative to speculative investments. During one cycle of the economy these investments may appear to be conservative, but then during the next cycle they appear to be speculative.

Undeveloped Land (Income 0-2)(Growth 6-7)(Risk 3-4)

During the highly inflationary seventies, farmland and other undeveloped properties were good investments. People speculated in land just as they did in income properties. This drove prices up and, unfortunately, tempted even farmers to speculate.

The eighties saw inflation subside and land prices level out. Consequently, raw land prices also fell. Today an investment in raw land is considered fairly conservative, although there is a risk if the purchase is leveraged. The prospect of the kind of growth seen in the seventies and eighties is considered unlikely, but this scenario can and will change again as the economy changes.

Housing (Income 5-7)(Growth 0-5)(Risk 3-4)

As noted previously, no investment during the last 25 years has been consistently better for the average investor than single-family rental houses. That doesn't mean that residential properties will appreciate the way they did over the last two decades, but I can see no long-range trends away from rental housing in the next decade. In fact, with the Tax Reform Act making multi-family housing less attractive to investors, fewer apartments will probably be built during the nineties. That should place more value on rental housing.

Housing costs are out of the price range of most average young couples, and since they have to live somewhere, most of them are going to rent, at least temporarily.

One advantage of investing in rental housing is that it can be done with a relatively small initial down payment. When investing in rental properties, the most important principle to remember is: no surety. If the house won't stand as collateral for its own mortgage, pass it by.

Rental housing not only generates income but also shelters much of that income through depreciation, interest, and taxes. The 1986 Tax Reform Act placed limits on what can be deducted for tax purposes against ordinary income, and it's entirely possible that future tax changes will affect real property even more. But I still believe rental housing promises good growth through the end of this century, barring an economic catastrophe.

On the other hand, there are several negatives to consider before investing in rental housing. (1) If you don't want to be a landlord, don't buy rental housing. (2) If you aren't able to maintain and manage your own property, many of the benefits decline. (3) It's not always easy to get your money out if you need it.

An option to investing in single-family rental housing is to invest in duplexes and triplexes. If you don't have the money to get into a duplex or triplex by yourself, there are two alternatives. You can invest in limited partnerships offered by individuals who purchase and manage duplexes and triplexes, or you can invest with another person. Since I have discussed both of these options earlier I won't elaborate again. The key factor to keep in mind is: The managing partner has total control. The advantage of owning a duplex or triplex is that your income isn't limited to one renter. In a single-family home, if your renter moves out, you have 100 percent vacancy. But in a duplex you would still have a 50-percent occupancy.

The liabilities with duplexes and triplexes are that they require a bigger investment and more maintenance, and you really do become a landlord.

Remember the three key factors about buying any rental property, whether it is a single-family house, duplex, or triplex: *location, location, location.*

Mutual Funds (Income 6-8)(Growth 4-5)(Risk 4-5)

A mutual fund is an investment pool for many small investors. A group of professional advisors invests for them, usually in the stock or bond markets. There are specialized mutual funds that invest in automobiles, precious metals, utility companies, government securities, and so forth. In fact, you can find a mutual fund for almost any area in which you want to invest.

Mutual funds are valuable for the small investor for several reasons. (1) You can invest with a relatively small amount of money (many mutual funds require as little as $500). (2) Your money is spread over a large area in the economy. (3) The return on the best mutual funds has averaged more than twice the prevailing interest rates for any 10-year period.

I would encourage any potential investor in mutual funds to go to independent sources and check out the fund first. Several sources are listed in the Appendix. Since we are discussing growth mutual funds, it is important to verify the track record and projected earnings of any fund you might select. A prospectus from the mutual fund company will clearly define the "secure" or low-risk funds and the "growth" or speculative funds.

I prefer to use no-load (non-commission) funds, because they allow my money to grow without the service fees or commissions coming out of the initial investment. No-load funds normally do not carry penalties if you decide to withdraw your money.

TIER 4:
SPECULATIVE INVESTMENTS

Common Stocks/Mutual Funds (Income 2-8)(Growth 0-7)(Risk 7-8)

Again, the advantages of common stocks are that you can invest with a relatively small amount of money and potential exists for sizable growth. The liabilities of common stocks are obvious. First, you can suffer a loss as easily as you can make a profit. Second, stocks require buying and selling to maximize their potential and consequently require broker fees. If you expect to make money in common stocks, you're probably going to have to trade them periodically. If you're not willing to do that, it's better to stick with other kinds of investments.

Precious Metals (Income 0)(Growth 0-8)(Risk 8-9)

As mentioned before, precious metals such as gold, silver, or platinum can be purchased either for long-term growth or pure speculation. For long-term growth, buy the metal, put it in a safety deposit box, and hope it appreciates over a period of time. Most people do this primarily as a hedge against a potential calamity in the economy. In an economy as unstable as ours, a small percentage of your assets invested in precious metals can help to balance other assets more vulnerable to inflation. When buying and selling anything, especially precious metals, it's wise to remember what Baruch said: "Buy when they sell. Sell when they buy." Keep a long-term mentality about precious metals—at least those you invest in as a hedge.

Both gold and silver fluctuate with the economy. Gold usually cycles faster and further than silver, primarily because more people trade in it. In general, the cycles of gold run the opposite of the U.S. dollar, so watch the dollar's trends for clues to the price of gold.

Other speculative investments include limited partnerships, syndications, penny stocks, and collectibles. It is virtually impossible to assign a rating to these since they vary so greatly, depending on the investor's expertise. Suffice it to say that the risks are great and so are the potential returns.

The reason that many of these investments are shown in both the speculative and high-risk categories is because they fall into either, depending on what the economy is doing at the time.

TIER 5:
HIGH-RISK INVESTMENTS

These investments should play only a relatively small part (5 to 10 percent at the most) in any investment plan. Their primary value is the potential appreciation; in other words, speculation. Most generate little or no income and are highly volatile.

Gold/Silver (Income 0)(Growth 0-10)(Risk 9-10)
Not only can you invest in precious metals for long-term growth, but you can also invest in gold and silver for short-term speculation. This would be most beneficial in a highly volatile economy where major changes were occurring, such as the oil crisis in the mid-seventies or the run-up in silver prices in the late seventies.

Obviously, such events are difficult to predict and are extremely risky. They are for the investor with a strong heart and cash only. Unless you are a professional investor, this is probably not an area where you want to risk a lot of money.

Oil and Gas (Income 0-8)(Growth 0-10)(Risk 10+)
In the late seventies and early eighties when crude oil prices cycled up, oil and gas investments were the hottest things going. But many people who invested money in oil and gas did not understand the risks involved, and the vast majority lost their investments when the prices fell and marginal wells became unprofitable. A high degree of risk exists, particularly in oil exploration.

In an effort to reduce the risks, many people invested in oil and gas limited partnerships in known gas and oil fields. Not only did they lose their money on these investments, but they also discovered they were liable for environmental damages caused by the wells. This kind of an investment is not only very risky, but usually very expensive. I believe the income potential for oil and gas over the next two decades is excellent, but if you plan to invest in oil and gas, risk only a small portion of your assets and don't let anybody talk you into risking larger amounts.

Commodities Market (Income 0)(Growth 0-10)(Risk 10+)

Commodities speculation requires a relatively small dollar investment and can bring huge returns, primarily through the use of leverage. As noted previously, a $1,000 investment in the commodities market can control $10,000 worth of contracts—or more—for future delivery. If that sounds good, remember this: "A fool and his money are soon parted." Approximately 1 out of every 200 people who invest in the commodities market ever gets *any* money back. That doesn't mean a profit; that means *any* money back. Investing in commodities is probably the closest thing to gambling that most Christians ever try. In fact, it *is* gambling. You can lose everything you own, and even more.

Collectibles (Income 0)(Growth 2-10)(Risk 10+)

Antiques, old automobiles, paintings, figurines, etc., are all collectibles that can be used while you hold them to sell. One of the most important prerequisites to investing in collectibles is *knowledge*. You need to know value before investing. Second, you need to put some time and labor into locating the best places to buy and sell. Third, you must have the capital to wait for just the right buyer. Often novice investors get discouraged and sell out at a loss.

Unless you have a high degree of knowledge in this area, the risk is inordinately high. With most items like antiques, automobiles, figurines, and paintings, you can develop the expertise you need by talking with other people and reading key periodicals. The rate of return on collectibles can easily be 10+, but the risk of loss is just as great.

Precious Gems (Income 0)(Growth 0-4)(Risk 10+)

Diamonds, opals, rubies, sapphires, and other stones can be purchased for relatively small amounts of money. Then they can be mounted into a ring or pendant and worn while you're waiting for them to appreciate. In my opinion, gem investors should consider this their best use. For every person I know who made money in gems, I know a hundred who lost money. As stated earlier, it's almost impossible for a novice to know the true value of a gem, even with a "certified" appraisal. Worst of all, it's very difficult to sell gems at a fair price unless you have your own market. The rule here is to stay with what you know or with someone you thoroughly trust.

Limited Partnerships (Income 0-7)(Growth 0)(Risk 10+)

Limited partnerships are formed to pool investors' money to purchase assets, usually in real properties. The investment is managed by a general partner who has the decision authority for buying and selling. Since your investment in a limited partnership is no better than the property and the management, the key is to know the general partner and his credibility.

A limited partner's liability is normally limited only to the amount of money at risk. Limited partnerships requiring subsequent annual payments or operating loss guarantees, or carrying contingent tax liabilities, should be avoided. Limit your liability to only the money you have at risk.

In the past, limited partnerships in properties, such as apartment complexes, office complexes, or shopping centers, were purchased primarily to shelter ordinary income. However, since 1987 most of these benefits have been gradually eliminated, and the tax write-offs can be used only to shelter passive income. For most investors, the risk is too high and the returns too uncertain.

This basic review of the five major types of investments is by no means exhaustive, but I trust it will provide you with the pointers to get started in an investment strategy once you have your budget under control and develop a surplus.

HOW THE TIERED APPROACH CAN WORK

Let's walk through five examples of how different investors might tier their investments to meet their goals.

1. *A widow, age 68, with $130,000 in cash to invest.* Her goals are to supplement her Social Security income by $500 a month, and leave her estate to her children upon her death.

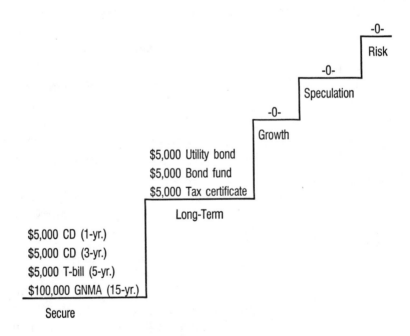

Total Return = **$10,000/year**

As you can see, her strategy is weighed heavily toward the low-risk tiers because she can meet all of her goals without assuming any significant risk. Her investments also provide her with adequate liquidity in the event she needs cash for medical expenses or other emergencies.

In the event that inflation picks up and begins to erode her assets, most of them are renewable in five years or less so she can reinvest at higher interest rates when necessary.

2. A 36-year-old physician with an income in the $150,000-a-year range. Goals: To become debt-free (medical school loans, office loans, and home loan), start a college fund for his children, and begin a retirement plan. He has $25,000 a year to invest after making required payments on indebtedness.

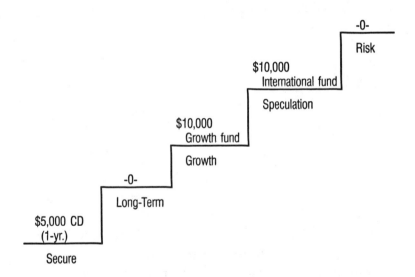

His primary investments are in mutual funds, divided between U.S. growth stocks and international stocks, for his children's eventual education. Other than a normal amount of emergency savings, his investment money is better used in retiring debt at this point in his career. His strategy should change between ages 40 and 60, then again at 60-plus.

3. *A car manufacturer employee with $30,000 to invest at age 62.* Goals: To retire this year on Social Security and company retirement income of approximately $2,000 per month combined, to use his surplus savings for travel and additional spending that his retirement income will not allow.

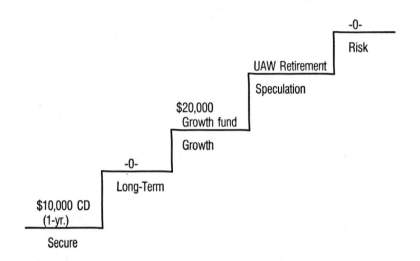

I have mapped this man's retirement account as a part of his investment program because it is, even though he has virtually no control over it. The $30,000 savings is divided into emergency savings and growth income. His risk is slightly higher than would be normal for a 62-year-old with limited assets, but since he does not require the funds to live on, he can maximize the return without too much risk. His average annual yield should be 10 to 12 percent.

4. *A 50-year-old manager of a municipal power company with $100,000 to invest from an inheritance.* Goals: To be debt-free by 62 and retire to work with his church. He and his wife have no children, owe $60,000 on their home, and have no other debts. He has an additional $800 a month to invest toward his retirement goals.

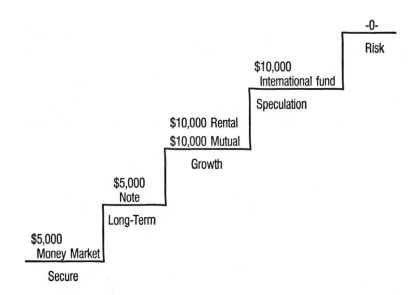

You will notice an obvious absence of $60,000 from this investment plan because they used that sum from the $100,000 inheritance to eliminate their home mortgage. The strategy is to reinvest the mortgage money in good quality mutual funds monthly.

The $40,000 they have to invest is placed in the middle risk/return tiers. They are seeking modest growth without excessive risk. This plan should return approximately 8 to 10 percent a year, providing a savings of approximately $200,000 (including the monthly investments) by age 62.

5. *A 52-year-old executive with $300,000 to invest, and approximately $100,000 per year in surplus income; no debts, college already provided for their children, and no specific retirement plans.* Goals: To multiply their assets to be able to give to missions work in Central America above the $100,000 they presently give.

Since this individual obviously doesn't need the surplus to live on, and since he has the ability to generate a sizable

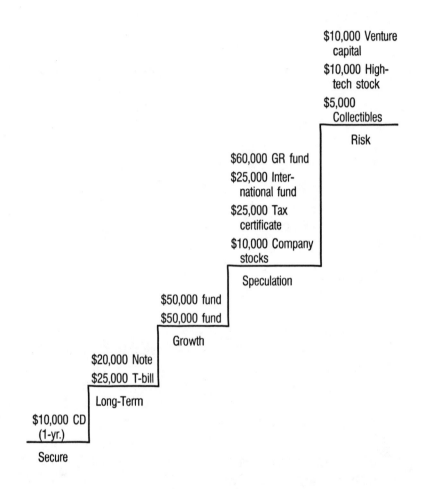

surplus annually, he decided to place most of the funds in the upper tiers for maximum return. He used the fifth tier, but avoided the very high-risk areas like precious metals and commodities. Since adopting this plan, he has earned approximately 25 percent annually on his investments. He has kept his asset level at approximately $200,000 and has given the rest away annually.

I need to make one point clear before closing this chapter.

You don't necessarily need to lay out your financial goals in a tier plan. I do this because it makes the examples simpler. The principle is the same whether you diagram or write out your goals: *You need to make very specific plans if you ever hope to accomplish them.* Both spouses need to discuss their long-range goals, and commit them to prayer. Until you do, why should you believe that God will entrust more to you? As Jesus said in Luke 16:10, "He who is faithful in a very little thing is faithful also in much; and he who is unrighteous in a very little thing is unrighteous also in much." Manage well the portion that you now have and God will be able to entrust even more to you.

15

Evaluating Cash Investments

O n the surface, deciding where to put your cash would not seem very complicated. But based on the amount of money still stored in passbook savings accounts I would surmise that many people don't realize there are better ways to invest their cash reserves. For instance, the same bank that pays 6 percent for money saved in a passbook account usually offers a money market account paying 1 to 2 percent more interest with almost exactly the same terms and safety. A phone call is all that is necessary to make the transfer. So why doesn't everyone do it? Most don't know they can.

Even the decision about whether to keep surplus funds in a checking account to qualify for free checking services can often be confusing. If a bank offers free checking for deposits of $1,000 or more and you write at least 40 checks per month at an average cost of 15 cents per check ($6 a month) you would have to earn over 7 percent interest (tax-free) in a savings account to match the earning on your $1,000 in the checking account. Also, many banks now pay interest on checking accounts with more than a $1,000 average monthly balance, so the benefit is increased even more. Some will say, "The amount of money is insignificant." Those who believe that are too rich!

I can assure you that based on the amount of money banks and brokerage firms spend advertising their cash accounts, they don't consider this decision inconsequential. The competition in CDs is fierce. I can also assure you that much of what you see is purposely confusing. I spent a few minutes recently calling several banks about their cash deposits and found that the rates were flexible, depending on who I talked to. The terms for early withdrawal, borrowing against the deposit, and even how the interest was calculated and paid varied from bank to bank.

In the end, I found my best return was a large brokerage firm's money market account in government securities. I beat the banks' best rate by a full percentage point and had no withdrawal restrictions on my (imaginary) funds. So clearly it is best to shop, even when looking for a cash savings account. This is especially true when placing sums of $10,000 or more.

BANK SAVINGS

The majority of American investors still keep their cash reserves in banks. Total cash reserves in banks as of 1991 were nearly twice that of all other consumer accounts at brokerage firms, credit unions, etc. Cash deposit accounts at banks can be broken down into three basic categories:

Passbook Accounts

These are unrestricted accounts that usually pay the minimum amount of interest, while allowing the depositor daily access to the funds. Usually a transaction fee is levied if the account is used more than a few times each month. The only advantage I can see with these accounts is that they will allow deposits as little as $10. Once the minimum amount necessary to qualify for a money market account is reached, the funds should be transferred.

Money Market Accounts

These can go under a variety of titles such as "Golden Passbook," "Ready Cash Account," "Preferred Investors Account," and so on. Usually they offer check writing privileges on amounts of $500 or more, and many banks also offer free cashier's checks, travelers' checks, even special loan rates to depositors. These accounts were established to compete directly with the brokerage firms' accounts that were attracting much of the small depositors' cash in the early eighties. The rates they offer are usually directly related to the brokerage firms' rates. Depositors can withdraw their funds without penalty at any time.

Certificates of Deposit

These are time deposit accounts that can vary from as short as three months to several years. Usually the longer the time and the larger the deposit, the higher the interest rate paid.

Usually there is a penalty for early withdrawal of funds, although the interest can sometimes be withdrawn without penalty. The Certificate of Deposit is probably the best known and most widely used of all the cash accounts, primarily because of the extensive advertising done by banks.

All three types of the aforementioned bank accounts are covered by the Federal Depositors Insurance Corporation (FDIC) up to the prescribed amounts (presently $100,000) in a single bank. As of this writing, accounts in different banks are insured separately. So you could have three deposits of $100,000 each in three different banks and each account be insured to the maximum amount. This is almost certain to be changed in the future to limit the maximum insurance on a combination of all FDIC accounts.

A significant liability of these cash accounts is that any income is taxable as it is earned, unless it is held in a qualified retirement account.

BROKERAGE FIRM ACCOUNTS

Most major brokerage firms offer a variety of cash investments, including the resale of most local, state, and federal government loans. Usually brokerage firms are the primary buyers of initial government loan offerings, which are then resold for a small percentage increase on the open market.

Perhaps the most common type of brokerage firm account is the money market fund. These are mutual funds that allow the participants to withdraw their cash as needed. Many money market funds provide check-writing privileges for the investors. Usually shares are offered for $1 apiece and the fund maintains that value. In other words, if you buy into the fund at $1 per share you can get out at $1 per share. Many people who use these funds don't realize that they are mutual funds, not savings accounts. There is no guarantee that the fund will repay dollar for dollar. So far the major funds have always repaid investors at par value, but nothing in the investment world is guaranteed.

Varieties of options exist even within the money market funds. Some funds invest only in short-term government loans, some specialize in business loans, etc. The interest they pay usually directly reflects the risk they take with your investment dollars. When a fund promises a higher than average rate of interest, you can be certain that there is a commensurately higher degree of risk.

If you have any concern about the safety of your funds, you would be better off leaving your cash reserves in an insured account.

CREDIT UNIONS

The growth of credit unions in the United States has been significant over the last two decades. These institutions offer savings accounts to their members that usually pay 1 to 2 percent higher rates of interest than other commercial institutions, such as banks. At one time the credit unions were rated as higher risks because they were insured by private underwriters, rather than the FDIC. In light of liabilities assumed by the FDIC over the last two decades, however, the credit unions are probably as good or better risk than FDIC banks, in my opinion.

If you invest with a credit union, be certain the institution is a member of the National Association of Credit Unions, is covered by their approved insurance program, and is fiscally sound.

INSURANCE COMPANIES

For more than 100 years insurance companies have been used as repositories for long-term savings. In the past the interest paid on cash values in insurance plans was meager but dependable. Throughout the Great Depression of the thirties when hundreds of banks failed, no major insurance company defaulted on its financial obligations, an admirable track record.

However, these are not the thirties, and insurance companies are not as stable as they were in past decades. Because of intense competition for investment dollars, insurance companies have been forced to increase their returns, and to do so they have taken on more risk themselves. Many large insurance companies have seen their ratings fall because of too much debt and too many bad investments (such as junk bonds).

As I said earlier, I believe you should look at insurance as provision in the case of premature death, not as an investment. The cash reserves in your policies can be used as emergency funds, but remember that loans against the policy reduce the death benefit to your dependents. The use of insurance products as investments is discussed in a later chapter.

16

Evaluating
Bond Investments

Most Americans invest in a bond at one time or another during their lives. It may be a U.S. savings bond offered by their employer, or money from their 401-K retirement account loaned to their company. Few investors realize that even the cash reserves in their insurance policies are often invested in bonds. Unfortunately the individual investor seldom has a voice in which bonds protect the money in insurance policies; and recently many have lost their savings in over-leveraged corporate bonds, the so-called "junk bonds."

Bonds form the backbone for most long-range financial planning; therefore it is critical to select them carefully, especially in the 60-plus stage of your financial life.

BONDS AND BOND FUNDS

Bonds
Bonds are the primary obligation of the issuer. The issuer can be an individual, a business, or a local, state, or federal government. Most brokerage firms sell bonds (and bond funds) for a small fee. The interest promised on any bond is directly related to three basic factors: the length of deposit, the amount invested, and the rating of the bond issuer.

It is arguable that some corporate bonds are probably safer than many government bonds. A major corporation like IBM may well be more solvent than a municipality like New York or Philadelphia. Actually a company, such as IBM, is probably sounder than the federal government, although the federal government does have the unique ability to print money.

Usually an investment in a specific bond is for a predetermined period of time. Thus the principal invested is not readily available unless the bond is resold. The face value of a bond can fluctuate according to the prevailing interest rates. For instance, if you purchase a bond for $1,000 paying 10 percent interest and the market rate drops to 8 percent, your bond will probably go up in value. If the prevailing market rate climbs to 12 percent, the bond value will probably drop. The actual increase or decrease in value is what makes the bond market volatile. As discussed previously, it is also what tempts the commodities dealers to gamble on the future value of bonds.

Bond Funds

Bond funds represent the best option for the majority of average investors, in my opinion. The diversification they offer helps to lessen the fluctuations in value and risk. Most bond funds also offer the option of buying and selling the shares without the penalty an ordinary bond would carry. It is important to select the bond funds with the same degree of caution that you would a specific bond. The security and dependability of the fund is directly related to where the fund invests its assets. For maximum safety, select the all-government fund. For higher income, select the corporate fund. For maximum income (and risk), funds made up of repurchased junk bonds, Third World debt, etc., are available.

Bonds are rated according to a complex formula that takes into account the company's (or government's) projected ability to repay under the most adverse of circumstances. These ratings from the rating services (see Appendix) change regularly if the risk of the bond issuer changes. The best bonds, and bond funds, carry a AAA rating. The riskiest carry a C rating or less. For the average investor, any bond or bond fund with a rating of less than AA should be considered risky. Most of the financial analysts I spoke with about rating services tended to depend more on the Standard and Poor's service because of the way they gathered the data on the bond issuers. For an interested investor, this information is available by subscribing to one of the bond-related newsletters.

Zero Coupon Bonds

Zero coupon bonds have become increasingly popular with investors over the last several years, particularly for funding education needs. A zero coupon bond is actually a note issued by a company or government agency at a discount. For instance, a 10-year bond with a redemption value of $1,000 may be sold to an investor for $700. No interest or dividends are paid during the period between issue and maturity (hence the term "zero coupon"). A more traditional bond contains interest-bearing coupons that can be clipped and redeemed during the holding period.

Depending on the type of zero coupon bond (or bond fund), the appreciated value of the bond is taxable income to the holder in each year. Hence a $1,000 bond, sold for $700 initially with a three-year maturity, would have taxable income assessed in each of the three years. This can create a tax problem unless the investor has the cash reserves necessary to pay the taxes. Some limited-issue zero coupon bonds are taxable only upon maturity. Usually these pay a slightly lower rate of interest because of this feature. Consult with your bond salesman before purchasing either type of bond. The same ratings apply to zero coupon bonds as with other types of bonds.

Government Bonds

There are three basic types of cash investments marketed directly by the federal government: savings bonds, Treasury bills (T-bills), and Treasury bonds.

SAVINGS BONDS. Savings bonds are loans to the government

for a predetermined period of time (usually seven years or longer). They were designed primarily to help fund the U.S. involvement in World War II, and were originally called "war bonds." Since the government hates to stop any program once started, the bond program was continued after the war and retitled "savings bonds."

Since savings bonds are loans made directly to the government, they are considered very secure. Savings bonds have one additional benefit in that the interest earned is not taxed until the bond is redeemed at maturity. Savings bonds, like most time deposits, carry a significant penalty for early redemption.

Savings bonds can be purchased in denominations as small as $25, which makes them available to most smaller investors. In 1990 a Series EE bond was introduced that allows the interest to go untaxed when used for the college education of the investor's dependent (under certain conditions). If you want a more detailed explanation of U.S. savings bonds, refer to the newsletters listed in the Appendix.

TREASURY BILLS. These are also loans made directly to the U.S. government. They can be purchased in small denominations for periods ranging from a few months to several years. The interest they pay depends on prevailing market conditions, but it is usually about 1 percent less than the interest paid on an equivalent bank CD because the federal government is considered a lower risk.

TREASURY BONDS/NOTES. These are usually offered in larger denominations of $25,000 or more, and for periods of up to 30 years. They constitute the government's basic method of financing its long-term debt. The interest rates vary with the prevailing markets, but usually are at least 1 percent lower than equivalent bank CDs and several percentage points lower than the equivalent corporate bonds.

Ginnie Maes

Ginnie Maes are bonds issued by the Government National Mortgage Association, and are actually a composite of mortgage loans guaranteed by the federal government and resold to the public. Ginnie Maes can be purchased in units of $10,000 or more, normally with an average maturity at the time of this writing of about 12 years. Other government agencies also back loan fund bonds, such as the Student Loan Marketing Association (Sallie Maes), and the Federal National Mortgage Association (Fannie Maes); all offer higher rates of interest with slightly more risk than other government debt.

The single largest negative of bonds like Ginnie Maes is that the borrowers have the option to prepay their loans at any time. So although you may purchase a Ginnie Mae bond expecting to receive your prescribed interest for the term of the bond, if the interest rates drop and the borrower elects to refinance and thus pays off your bond, you have no option. You may well find yourself trying to reinvest your funds at substantially lower interest rates.

Some municipal loan programs for poor and lower income families are backed by government bond programs such as Ginnie Mae. These bonds provide tax-exempt income for the investors, but usually carry a lower rate of interest. Quotes can be obtained from any bond broker.

TAX CERTIFICATES

A little-known and seldom utilized type of bond is a municipal tax certificate. A tax certificate is actually a lien placed on a taxpayer's property for delinquent taxes by a municipality (state, county, city, etc.).

In virtually all municipalities, property taxes are assessed and payments required annually. If the taxes are not paid within a prescribed period, a lien is placed on the property, and a tax certificate is issued that is then sold at public auction.

The buyer (lender) of a tax certificate is legally the lienholder on the property. If the certificate is not repaid with the accumulated interest before the statute of limitations for tax liens expires (three years in most states), the lender can foreclose on the property, thereby assuming all the rights of the property owner.

The interest rate assigned to tax certificates is usually significantly higher than the prime interest rate. Keep in mind the rule of risk and return. The reason the rate is higher is the inherent risk involved. When you purchase a tax certificate you can acquire no greater rights than the taxpayer. If there is an outstanding mortgage, you must assume that loan. If the property has a title flaw, you will assume that too. It is important to investigate carefully the collateral backing the certificate you purchase. Information on tax certificates can be obtained from most county tax offices.

CHURCH BONDS

I have included this category of bonds because of their prevalence in the Christian community. These are loans made to a church (normally) to fund a building program. Two significant points need to be made here:

1. *It is my conclusion, based on my study of God's Word, that loans to Christians (and Christian organizations such as a church) should be made without interest.* If you would like to study this topic for yourself, I would direct you to the following Scriptures: Leviticus 25:35-37, Deuteronomy 23:19-20, Nehemiah 5:7-10, and Psalm 15:5. (There are several other references about lending without interest to God's people, but these will give you an overview.) Then you must decide for yourself whether or not you believe this principle is applicable to God's people today; personally, I do.

2. *Church bonds are high-risk loans and should be made only out of surplus funds that you can afford to lose if necessary.* I have counseled many Christians, including retirees and widows, who loaned money to a church bond program that they should not have risked. Several lost their entire savings believ-

ing they were helping God's work and He would protect them. As best I can tell from God's Word, He is not in the lending business. When you lend, you're on your own.

JUNK BONDS

Junk bonds is a term used to describe many of the bonds that were used to finance leveraged buyouts of companies during the eighties. They are usually collateralized only by the good will of the issuer, and carry much higher than average interest rates.

Since the demise of the junk bond market in the early nineties, few new junk bonds have been issued or offered. However, many previously issued junk bonds are still floating around and are regularly resold to gullible investors. There are even junk bond funds established for the sole purpose of investing in these highly risky ventures. The high returns blind many investors who are foolish enough to think they can "beat the system."

UTILITY BONDS

The public utility companies throughout the country often finance new construction projects through long-term bonds. Over the last two decades, utility bonds (and stocks) have become the backbone of many investment plans. The advantages they offer are stability and relatively high interest rates.

However, utility bonds are not without risk themselves. Many investors who risked their money with utility companies in the seventies and eighties to build nuclear power facilities got a rude surprise as established utility companies defaulted on payments. Cost overruns and government regulations simply made many of these projects unprofitable. Although utility companies operate under a public utility license, they still must make a profit to repay creditors. Those that don't, can't.

Except for the bonds associated with nuclear power devel-

opment, utility bonds have been rated among the best investments in America for nearly 70 years. For the average investor, the purchase of a utility bond fund probably makes more
sense because the risk can be spread over many utility companies. The evidence of this logic can be seen in the fact that
even when individual utility companies were defaulting on
bonds attached to nuclear power facilities, the utility bond
funds were still paying their investors. It is the simple principle
of diversification.

MUNICIPAL BONDS

Local municipalities can issue interest-bearing bonds that are
exempt from federal income taxes. Many states exempt the
interest on bonds issued by municipalities within the state
from state income taxes as well.

Because of this tax-exempt feature, municipal bonds are
popular with higher income investors. However, it is easy to be
beguiled by the promise of tax-free income. If you decide to
invest in municipal bonds, or bond funds, you need to verify
the rating of the issuing municipality. Several large cities are
on the verge of insolvency and are able to pay the interest on
existing bonds only by selling more bonds. This is very similar
to a pyramid scheme in which only the early participants can
get their money back. We have yet to see a major municipality
default in our present generation. But I assure you, municipal
bond holders during the Depression saw many municipalities
default.

Also bear in mind that if your total tax rate is 40 percent, a
totally taxable bond yielding 10 percent is the same as a tax-
exempt bond yielding 6 percent. It may well be that the 10-
percent bond is a better buy when risk is factored in.

17

Evaluating Stocks and Stock Funds

T
he process of buying and selling stocks is probably the most visible area of investing to the average American. Stock market quotes are given on virtually every news program, and changes in the Dow Jones stock index make every major network's news. In recent years violent swings up and down in the market indexes have almost numbed the average American to what they really indicate. The market no longer reflects the true value of a company's worth. Rather it reflects the current mood of those who buy and sell stocks and bonds. With the advent of the large institutional investors (mutual funds and pension funds), relatively few traders can cause huge swings in the market. As the downturn of the market in October 1987 demonstrated, computer-originated trading can actually cause a market collapse if left unattended by human rationale.

What actually happened that fateful day in October (by most accounts) was that the automated trade programs, designed to minimize losses, were triggered to initiate sell orders by a sudden downturn in the indexes they monitor. These sell orders in turn triggered more trading by other programs and the big sell-off was in progress. By the time anyone realized what was happening and unplugged their computers, the biggest one-day drop in the history of the market had occurred. Subsequent changes in the way these programs function have made similar sell-offs unlikely. But without a doubt, something equivalent will occur in the future as stock market trading gets more sophisticated and volatile.

I say this only to warn you again that trading in stocks (and stock funds to a lesser degree) is highly speculative. Stocks should be used only as growth investments for the prere-tirement years, or for surplus funds after retirement. The use of mutual funds can help to reduce the risk associated with stock trading, but nothing can eliminate it.

I found in my reading that most secular investment books have some excellent sections and some so totally contrary to God's principles that they negate the worth of the good parts. Consistently, the one area most of them are off base is that of stock speculation. The authors of investment books are com-monly stock salesmen (and women) who have made a great deal of money themselves by selling stocks. Just remember, a significant difference exists between investing in stocks and selling them. The broker makes money whether we do or not.

I found two consistent flaws in the advice given by most of the writers who also sell stocks for a living. First, they recommended the use of debt to invest. Second, they use stocks as their prima-ry investments to the exclusion of less risky investments.

DISCOUNT BROKERS

As stated previously, discount brokerage firms place orders; they do not provide investment advice. When using a discount broker you must know what stocks, bonds, or other invest-ments you want to buy. The broker simply places your order and charges a small fee for the service. Usually the fee is a small percentage of what a standard broker charges.

Probably the most widely known discount firm is Charles Schwab and Associates. This company started the current trend toward a nationwide use of discount brokerage firms in the early seventies. For stock or bond investors who need placement services only, a discount broker, like Schwab, can significantly reduce their trading costs.

The argument for using a discount broker is purely economic. More of your investment dollar goes into the investment. The argument against using a discount broker is that you receive no counsel when investing. In general, the decision to use or not to use discount services should be based on your ability to make investment decisions. If you don't need advice, why pay for it? If you do, the fee should be worth what you pay. The bottom line is, a fee-based broker should make you more than his fees cost you.

BLUE CHIP STOCKS

The so-called "Fortune 500" companies are often referred to as the blue chips (an obvious association with the higher value chips used on the tables in Las Vegas). These are some of the largest companies listed on the stock exchange, and represent the base value of American industry.

If an investor had simply spread his stock investments over the blue chip companies (or the Dow Jones list of companies used to establish the daily index) for the last 10 years, he would have earned approximately 10 percent annually (after inflation) in growth and dividends. There would have been some bad moments when it looked like the market would collapse as it did in the thirties, and nothing says it won't in the future, but overall, stocks were a better than average investment. It is the risk that makes them so volatile for the average investor, and the fact that outside of a balanced mutual fund it is difficult for most people to invest in a wide enough base of companies to lower the risk.

Normally good quality stocks are divided into two broad categories by investment analysts: *growth* and *income*.

Growth stocks are usually associated with newer companies, or emerging technologies. IBM was considered a growth stock in the early fifties. Xerox was a growth company in the sixties. Texas Instruments was a growth company in the seventies.

Apple Computers became a growth company in the eighties. In the nineties the growth industry will probably be health-related companies. In the next century environmental companies could very well lead the way.

This does not mean that once a company has been a "growth company" that the stock does not appreciate. IBM is a good example of a company that has seen a steady growth pattern for more than three decades. But compared to the company's early days it would now be considered a stable income company.

Income stocks are selected primarily because of their stable, long-term income through dividends. Good examples of this type of investment would be utility stocks, automobile stocks, defense industry stocks, and the like. Once a company has established a decade-long track record of paying regular dividends, many investors seek them as a means to earn both income (through dividends) and growth (through stock appreciation). Often a company that is noted for its dividend payout will see its stock prices fall rapidly if the dividend is less than projected. On the other hand, a company selected primarily for growth may see its stock appreciate even though the company never declares a dividend.

It is important that you know which category a company's stock fits into when making an investment. There are rating services that provide this information. Some of the better known are listed in the Appendix.

THE NEW YORK AND AMERICAN STOCK EXCHANGES

Most people know there are two stock exchanges, the New York and American, but don't know what the differences are. Both exchanges serve similar functions, but to vastly different sized companies. Generally the American Exchange offers a sales outlet for smaller, less established companies' stocks; the New York Exchange serves the country's biggest companies.

The exchanges are businesses run on a for-profit basis. They are not governmental agencies, nor are they affiliated with any agency of the government. Both are regulated by the Securities and Exchange Commission, which is an agency of the government, but only to control illegal actions that can adversely affect the public.

OVER-THE-COUNTER STOCKS

The cost of preparing a company's stock for sale on the national exchanges is prohibitively expensive for many emerging firms. In order for them to have a market for their stocks, the exchanges created the over-the-counter market. Stocks offered on this market are subject to less stringent Securities and Exchange rules as far as capitalization, income, and size are concerned. Basically these are speculative offerings of companies in the growth category. Buyers are presumed to be warned by the very fact that a stock is offered through the over-the-counter market.

Contained within this group of stocks are those often referred to as "penny" stocks. These probably represent the ultimate in risk of any stock regularly traded to the public.

The term *penny stock* refers to the very low price of the stocks, although not necessarily only pennies. When sales in these stocks began, the prices were actually a few pennies; since then the name has stuck. Investors in penny stocks should be advised that the risk is extremely high. These companies come and go regularly, rarely leaving any equity behind. The few that survive can appreciate greatly in value. But very few companies now traded on either exchange started as penny stock companies.

MUTUAL FUNDS

As previously discussed, a mutual fund is nothing more than a pooling of investors' money to purchase a cross section of stocks or bonds. Mutual funds gained popularity in the sixties, but really grew in popularity during the seventies. Where originally some 30 funds existed, there are now literally thousands of mutual funds offering wide diversification.

In order to attract investors in a very competitive field, mutual funds now offer a variety of options. One fund may offer investments ranging from growth stocks and blue chips to utilities, government bonds, and municipal bonds. When you invest in the fund you have the option of shifting or spreading your money into one or more of these areas without penalty. Most funds now allow investors to shift their funds within their "family" of investments once or twice a year without penalty. This offers maximum diversification even for small-dollar investors.

Since mutual funds are securities, they are normally sold through registered brokers. The fund company must also publish a prospectus showing the current financial condition of the fund, including administrative costs. Since the returns shown in the prospectus are historical only, it is important either to read the prospectus carefully or to subscribe to a service where a trained mutual fund expert does it for you. Such services are listed in the Appendix.

Past history is a good indication of what a fund has done, but it is not always a good indicator of what it will do in the future. A trained analyst can review a fund's performance and compare it with current management philosophy, cash position, and market position to come up with a reasonable projection of what the fund can do in the future. Never rely on a one-year performance record (and certainly not a one-quarter performance) when selecting a fund. It may well be that the managers guessed right in a given market and cannot duplicate the feat again.

LOADED VERSUS NO-LOAD FUNDS

We discussed this aspect of mutual funds earlier, but it is worth repeating one more time. A "loaded" fund is one in which a commission or sales charge is taken out of the funds invested before the fund units are purchased. For example, if you invested $1,000 in a fund whose units sell for $1 a share, and pay a 6-percent "load" or commission, you will own 940 shares.

A "no-load" fund has no commissions or sales charge taken out at the time of purchase, so you would own an additional 60 shares. No-load funds are sold exclusively by the fund company through direct solicitation. Since no commissions are paid, there are no local sales agents.

Whether a fund is a loaded or no-load has no real bearing on its performance. There are no-load funds listed among the top funds, and there are loaded funds in the top group also. It is important to select a good fund, regardless of how the fees are paid.

Given the fact that a good no-load fund can perform as well as a good loaded fund, I personally would rather invest in the no-load fund so that more of my money is working for me from the outset. "Net" return is the most important feature of any investment. It is critical to know how much the fund you select charges in annual administrative fees and commissions. There are many good fund rating services that evaluate net performance. You will find them listed in the Appendix under "Mutual Fund Services."

MARKET TIMING

In recent years a lot has been said about market timing in mutual funds. Market timing means that the funds are shifted from one type of investment to another depending on what's happening in the market. Or more correctly, what someone *thinks* will happen.

For instance, if a major downturn in the stock market is projected, it makes sense to shift from a growth fund to a government bond fund, thus avoiding the loss associated with the market downturn. Conversely, it also makes sense that when the market is projected to turn up again, the funds should be switched back to the growth fund.

During the eighties, dozens, perhaps hundreds, of these market timing services were started. Most evolved into newsletters and phone services that advised mutual fund investors when to switch from one type of fund to another. Some actually assumed the responsibility of switching the funds for investors.

More often than not, these timing services were started by a financial advisor who had gained notoriety by correctly projecting a major market move. Also more often than not, the feat was not repeated and the subsequent timing advice was usually inaccurate.

I asked several top financial advisors who have used these services at one time or the other how well they had done for them. The average was 25 percent right—about half of what flipping a coin would be. For the average investor, the cost of subscribing to such a service rarely is worth the benefit derived from it, in my opinion.

18

Investing in Real Estate

W ithout question, residential housing has been one of the most profitable areas of investment for most Americans over the last 40 to 50 years. The advent of the consumer credit boom that began after World War II provided the impetus for real estate appreciation, especially residential real estate. Simply put, more families were able to afford better housing through long-term financing.

The difficulty with any debt-financed expansion is that as the debt bubble expands it gets increasingly difficult to keep it inflated. The people who get in at the beginning make real profits since they can resell their expensive homes, move to a less expensive area of the country, and live on the surplus. But as the expansion continues there are fewer less expensive areas to move to and less appreciation in the existing homes. In a worst-case scenario the price of property drops as new buyers cannot manage the increasing monthly payments.

Once investors progress from residential real estate to other forms of real estate, such as commercial, farm land, and multi-family, the picture gets a lot cloudier. Some investors have done exceedingly well in high-growth areas like Florida and California. Others have done quite poorly in areas where the values rise and fall quickly. The oil patch in Texas and Oklahoma is a classic example of this fluctuating market. In these states, investing in real estate is much like investing in stocks;

if you hit the right market you can make a lot of money. But if you hit the wrong market you can lose it all—and then some.

What I would like to do is discuss briefly each area of real estate investing and share some insights from others who have done well.

RESIDENTIAL REAL ESTATE

There are no "magical" insights when it comes to investing in residential properties. The old adage in real estate is still true, "There are three important factors to consider when buying rental property—location, location, location."

The primary determinant of resale is where the property is located. Other factors are important, such as physical condition, price, even how a home smells. But these can all be corrected if necessary. Location is fixed and forever. Obviously if you buy for the long term, you also need to consider area trends. A neighborhood that is on the decline can destroy the value of homes in the area. Conversely, a neighborhood on the mend can add great value to the properties.

One major consideration before investing in rental properties is whether or not you have the temperament to be a landlord. If you don't have some maintenance ability, including some mechanical aptitude, I suspect you will not be happy owning rental property. Another factor is temperament. If you don't have the temperament to tell people they must vacate your property if they don't pay their rent, don't be a landlord. That may sound a little harsh, but I'll guarantee you that every landlord is eventually faced with that decision.

The general rule for investing in rental housing is that 11 months of rental income must be able to cover 100 percent of all expenses including payments, taxes, maintenance, and insurance. If it will not, normally it is not a good investment. This formula leaves one month per year that can be used for income, or vacancy.

The long-range strategy for investing in rental property

should be to have the property pay off the mortgage before you retire so that the income is available at retirement. A second alternative is to sell the property using owner financing. The mortgage payments then become a steady, dependable source of income after retirement.

In my opinion, the biggest drawback of investing in rental properties today is that virtually no commercial lenders will finance real estate without a personal guarantee on the loan. I would not give a personal endorsement (surety) for any loan. Therefore, unless I could find an owner-financed home, or borrow using only the property as collateral, I would not invest in rental housing (or anything else). When you borrow on surety you potentially risk everything you have accumulated to that point.

COMMERCIAL REAL ESTATE

For the vast majority of average investors, commercial real estate is beyond their financial resources, unless they pool their funds with other investors. I have already discussed the use of limited partnerships to do this in chapter 5, so I won't rehash that again. It is sufficient to say that unless you have a large degree of control over a project, you're generally better off pooling your investment money in a mutual fund where professional management is used.

From this point on, I will assume that those who will invest in commercial real estate have the financial ability to do so, and are not numbered among the fainthearted. If these two elements are present (money and courage), a great deal of money can be made in commercial real estate. A review of those who attempted to get rich quick in commercial real estate should be sobering enough to frighten most investors out of the commercial real estate market. I will not attempt to discuss the details of investing in one of Donald Trump's hotels, or investing in multi-story office buildings. If that is your investment strategy, you probably won't be helped by reading this book. I suggest a good book on psychiatry instead!

In reality there are only a few investments in commercial real estate available to average investors. I will briefly discuss some of the more common opportunities.

Storage Buildings

Some of the most profitable investments in commercial properties over the last 20 years have been mini-warehouse storage buildings. These are the small rental buildings used by many people for temporary storage space. The initial investment in these facilities is not insignificant. Often the cost of land, construction, and start-up advertising can run several thousand dollars per unit. But in good locations the storage units will repay all costs in five years or less. The obvious key is selecting the right location and analyzing the market carefully, including the competition.

I have a friend who has invested in mini-warehouse storage for nearly 15 years. All of his units repaid their total costs in six years or less, and now generate substantial cash flow for him. When he started he lacked the resources to buy the land and construct the storage facilities without going deeply into debt, which he had determined not to do. He solved the problem by forming a joint venture with some businessmen who had the funds to risk. He became the manager and part owner of the first several units, while they were basically silent partners. He located the properties, contracted for the construction, rented the units, and collected the monthly payments. For his partners, the storage units became their best investments ever, returning nearly 30 percent a year on their initial investments. As you would imagine he had no lack of willing partners, once the word got out.

Once he was established he was able to build more storage facilities using his own funds. In 15 years he has accumulated nearly $400,000 in paid-up units, generating almost $80,000 a year in income.

Since he lives in a recreational area, he has recently diversified into boat storage units located adjacent to a large nearby lake. The return per dollar invested is nearly twice that of ordinary storage units. It seems that American boat owners are attached to their pleasure crafts. It also seems only fitting that he is able to take some of that recreation money and put it back into the Lord's work.

Time-Share Condominiums

During the late seventies and eighties the concept of building condominium complexes in recreational areas and selling interests to multiple owners was hatched. The idea caught on with investors immediately, and time-shared condos sprung up in Florida (and elsewhere) like cabbage palms.

On the surface the idea was great. Why should vacationers tie up a lot of money in a cramped motel room when, for a small investment, they could own a share in a condo and rent it out when they didn't want to use it?

Difficulties surfaced as more and more units were constructed and the competition for renters grew so fierce that finding them required large advertising budgets and steep discounts. Since the rental agencies were not going to take the losses, the only logical prospects were the absentee owners. Many investors found themselves stuck with a condo they couldn't use, high annual mortgage payments, maintenance fees, and rental costs, not to mention declining income from their units.

When the tax laws changed so that the interest and depreciation could no longer be used to shelter other income, many investors tried to dump their shares, collapsing the resale market. Those who bought in during the collapse stage actually got some very good values for their investments. But overall, time shares have proven to be a very bad investment for the majority of buyers. Unless you really know what you're doing and can manage your own units in an area where you live, my counsel is to avoid them.

Lease-Repurchase Agreements

A popular concept that was developed in the eighties is selling rented office space to investors. I have several counselees who have invested in these situations and have done quite well. The concept is simple. A developer builds an office building and rents it out to qualified tenants. The rented offices are then resold to individual investors who become the owner/ landlords. Assuming the tenants are stable and dependable businesses, the arrangement works well for all parties. Often the tenant will sign a lease agreement with an option to buy at a later date. A good office building can yield an average return of 20 percent a year, or more.

The caution here is in qualifying the lease tenant. If the tenant cannot or will not pay the lease, the unit must be rented to another qualified tenant. Often that entails remodeling the offices to suit the next lessee. Unfortunately, the owner has to bear this cost.

As lease-repurchase agreements have grown in many areas of the country, the competition for good tenants has increased and revenues have declined. In short, this investment should be considered only with firsthand knowledge of the tenant. If you can't afford to pay cash for the unit, you should probably avoid this type of investment.

LAND SPECULATION

Virtually everyone in America knows of someone who struck it rich in the land business. Those who don't know someone certainly know someone who said they would have been rich had they just had the sense to invest in land 20 years ago. Tucked in the back of our minds somewhere is this secret desire to be one of those people who owned 10 acres in Kissimmee, Florida before Disney World came to town. I had a friend who owned 30 acres there and profited greatly. But it was purely by chance, not by design.

We both worked at the Kennedy Space Center in Florida,

long before Walt Disney ever thought about building his Magic Kingdom in central Florida. My friend got so tired of the stress that he decided to move to a quiet little community—Kissimmee—and start an antique car restoration business. Little did he know at the time he would relocate in the busiest community in America three years later. It worked out okay for him since he sold his property for slightly over $10 million more than his original purchase price of $20,000. Few people are so fortunate, but it is those who receive the publicity.

I heard my father tell the story about owning hundreds of acres in central Florida during the early twenties. He gave it back to the county when he had to start paying taxes on it. After all, who would want to pay taxes on virtually useless swampland?

These stories could be repeated by millions of Americans, and each time the consensus would be, "If I had only known then what I know now." Unfortunately that's true of any investment. Who would have believed in Edison's day that anyone would want a light bulb when there was no cost-effective way to power it? Besides that, gas lights worked just fine. For every one who invested in Edison's invention and prospered there were millions who lost money in ventures (land included) that looked more promising at the time.

With rare exception most people who invest in raw (undeveloped) land show very little return for their investment. Unless they can use the land themselves, the annualized rate of return when they sell is less than 5 percent a year. They would have done far better in a good stock fund over the same period of time.

If you are bound and determined to invest in raw land I would offer these suggestions:

1. *Buy only if you can see a future use for the property that will make it appreciate.* (For example, it's generally safe to buy raw land in a developing community where the property might eventually be going commercial or residential.)

2. *Plan to keep the property until it is totally paid off.* Don't

anticipate selling it before a balloon payment comes due. If you can't handle the payments until it is paid off, don't take the risk.

3. *Buy only if the property can be used as total collateral for the loan (no surety).* Usually this will require owner financing, since virtually no commercial lender will lend without a personal endorsement.

4. *Avoid joint ventures or partnerships to buy land.* Often what happens is the other parties can't pay their share and you will either have to pay the entire costs or forfeit your equity. Then not only is their credit rating blemished, but yours is too. As Proverbs 22:1 says, "A good name is to be more desired than great riches, favor is better than silver and gold."

19

Evaluating Collectibles and Precious Metals

I nvesting in collectibles (coins, stamps, cards, antiques, etc.) is clearly more of an art than a science. Often it is a matter of guessing what the other collectors want and finding the good deals before they do. If you can buy the right product at the right price, a profit can be made. But if you guess wrong, you probably made a purchase rather than an investment.

Investing in collectibles is not new. For centuries investors have purchased paintings and other forms of art, as well as furniture, dolls, toys, and books. In our generation the art of collectible investing has been brought to the level of a corporate enterprise. Major auctions are held regularly where anything from autos to baseball cards is offered. This publicized buying frenzy has driven up prices over the last decade, and there would appear to be no slackening in the foreseeable future.

Collectible investing truly is a worldwide market today. Any auction of significance will draw bidders from every part of the globe. If you have the right item at the right time, price is no object to many wealthy industrialists who have apparently run out of places to spend their money.

The real key to making money through collectibles is *expertise.* You must know what you're doing or someone who does will sell you the proverbial "pig in a poke." Before you decide to risk any of your money in collectibles, I would heartily encourage you to focus on one area (cards, stamps, etc.), read all you can about it, practice with "pretend" funds, and then start small.

Even though a collectibles salesperson professes to be a Christian and seems willing to offer you a good deal in his or her area of expertise, you need to know what you're doing. Usually I find that the people who are particularly good at what they do seldom need other investors. It is the people who sell investments for a living who offer the "good deals" to others. Unfortunately, many of them know only what they have been told, and that is just a little bit more than the people to whom they are selling. The more you know yourself, the easier it is to sort out the sheep from the goats.

I have known many people who have invested in collectibles. In general, I would categorize most of them as relatively successful. Usually the pattern was that they got started by buying from a professional. With rare exception they lost money on the "good deals" offered by the professionals. However, often this sparked an interest that developed into a hobby, and later into a business. So you could say the professionals helped launch their investment career in collectibles.

My observation is: Skip the losses and learn what you need to know first. Attend a few shows or auctions, read the best books available, and start small. You will be amazed how simple it is to become an expert in any one area.

COLLECTIBLES WITH ESTABLISHED MARKETS

Collectibles such as stamps, coins, sports cards, paintings, and antique furniture all have established markets, meaning that they are regularly traded through established outlets. Some are traded through auctions. Others are traded through trade shows. Still others are traded through magazines. Some are bought and sold through all of the above.

Having an established market outlet is a very important

consideration for the average investor because often it is much easier to buy a collectible than it is to sell one. You may invest in a fine crystal glassware set that has good potential, but unless you can find a willing and able buyer you may not be able to resell it. The law of supply and demand works in the collectible area just as it does in any other. The more people who regularly buy and sell collectibles, the higher the price can go (normally). The principle of supply and demand is simple: Increase the demand with a limited supply and the price will also increase.

Many excellent books are available on how to understand the area of collectibles. If you will invest a few dollars and a lot of time to study these carefully, you can avoid many of the hard lessons that come with losing money.

Nothing can replace an instinct for finding the good deals. Some people can read all the books ever written on buying and selling collectibles and still not have the knack for evaluating what is a good deal and what is not.

I have a friend who literally eats and sleeps with rare coins. He began collecting when he was about 12 and has been trading them ever since. For entertainment he goes to trade shows and barters coins. For reading material he scours the trade magazines. As a result, he has made a considerable fortune from rare coins.

You may not want to go to that extreme in your investing. But there are two things to remember: *first,* the more you know, the easier making money becomes; *second,* in any investment field there are people, like my friend, with whom you will be competing. He makes a large portion of his money off of novices who buy too high, panic when the market declines, and then want to sell quickly.

NON-MARKET COLLECTIBLES

Many collectibles either have no established market, or a very limited market. Such is the case with semiprecious stones.

There is a readily available market to purchase stones like topaz, aquamarines, and amethysts. Unfortunately, that market normally works only in one direction. In other words, the dealers will sell to the consumers, but won't buy from them.

When you invest in collectibles that have no ready market you must either make the market by advertising, selling to friends and family, or through some other means—or else you're stuck with the items and no way to get your money out.

My counsel is to avoid this type of collectible unless you truly know what you're doing and can market them yourself. I know someone who does just that. He shops estate sales, flea markets, garage sales, and any other source for collectibles with unique value. The items he buys may be anything from gems to historical memorabilia. He then ships them to another friend in California who has access to Hollywood celebrities where he sells them at outrageous prices to people who have more money than sense. He has made a market where none existed before, and profits handsomely from it.

NARROW MARKET COLLECTIBLES

This type of collectible includes investment-quality diamonds, works of art, historical documents, and the like. I term them narrow markets because an organized outlet usually exists but access to it is limited to a few select dealers and brokers. As I mentioned in an earlier chapter, when you risk your money in something like an investment-grade diamond you must be careful that you're not paying retail, because when you want to resell, the dealer will rarely pay above wholesale. There are collectors who will pay a fair price for such items, but usually they buy only through established dealers. So the average investor is excluded from access to the collectors except by random chance advertising.

I once counseled with a widow whose husband had invested in rare books for many years and owned a fine collection of original manuscripts by several well-known writers. Unfortunately, when she attempted to sell the collection, the dealers offered her only a fraction of what she knew their collector value was. But without their contacts she was unable to find qualified buyers.

Eventually a Christian friend helped her to market the collection in an ingenious way. He contacted the original publisher of some of the books, who was still in business, and asked if the company would be interested in buying the collection for display. They were, and she received an excellent offer. The remainder of the books was donated to a historical museum and the tax write-offs were enough to shelter most of the profit from the sale. The moral here is that God often intercedes to help widows. Foolish investors may not be so fortunate.

PRECIOUS METALS

The ownership of precious metals, particularly gold, has become as much of a controversy as the issue of whether to buy whole life or term insurance. What has created the controversy in precious metals is the radical movement that believes the economy will collapse and gold will be the salvation of all wealth.

In reality there is a lot of truth in that position. It is quite possible that our economy will collapse under the weight of its excessive debt burden. It is also possible that precious metals will appreciate in value greatly during that time. But the fallacy of that theory, in my opinion, is believing that gold or any other precious metal will become the principal means of transacting business. There is simply too little gold available and too much currency in circulation. It is more probable that the whole world's exchange system will become totally electronic, using no currency at all. At that point gold will become just another speculative commodity. Any long-term financial planning should include the purchase of some precious metals, but should never be weighed too heavily in balance with other investments (in my opinion). I would recommend limiting any investment in precious metals to around 5 percent, and certainly no more than 15 percent, of your total investment funds.

Buying and Selling Gold or Silver

I will limit the discussion of precious metals to only gold and silver since they are the most recognizable and regularly traded of all precious metals.

Both gold and silver are bought and sold by a variety of agents throughout the country. Some deal exclusively in precious metals, but most sell a variety of other investments as well. Because of the volatility of metals, most brokers have had to offer a variety of other products to keep their investor base. When the economy is unstable and metals are in vogue, dealers do quite well. But when the economy is growing, the metals market often turns down and most brokers find it difficult to earn a living. This is generally true with any investment products, but with precious metals the swings are wider, the peaks are shorter, and the down periods are longer. When the demand for precious metals is waning, it seems that gold salesmen use the fear mentality to promote gold as the panacea for all economic woes. I rather suspect this is more to drum up business in a down market than a conviction that gold really is the answer to a potential collapse.

When an investor buys gold or silver through an established broker, it is very much like buying a diamond through a retailer. In most instances the metal is being marketed at retail price. When investors attempt to resell they find that the dealers will offer only the current wholesale price or less. The difference can often amount to 15 percent on any given day. Obviously, if the price of gold or silver increases more than 15 percent (of retail), a profit is made. But more often than not an investor finds that although the price has increased, it is less than the difference between wholesale and retail. An even worse situation is to sell when the price drops below the original purchase price.

Time ✓159 no 4

p 24-7

Jan 28 2002

Daniel Kadlec

~~USA Today~~

Fortune ✓144 no 6

92-102

Oct 1 2001

Tully, Shawn

Gold and silver can be purchased directly from member brokers of the commodities exchange, as well as from dealers. Usually the broker requires a minimum purchase of several hundred dollars in the metal. The advantage in using a broker is that he or she usually charges a fixed rate above the wholesale price. This will vary per broker, but is normally significantly less than what a local dealer charges.

An alternative method of buying metals is through a discount broker. Discount brokers advertise in most investment magazines, as well as *The Wall Street Journal.* They will usually sell gold and silver for the current "ask" price quoted on the exchange, plus a nominal commission. Be sure if you buy through a discount broker that you take physical delivery of the metal. I have known several investors who opted to allow the broker to warehouse their purchase. Later, when they tried to recover their investment, they discovered the broker had closed shop and disappeared, along with their gold or silver. If you need to store the metal, use a bonded, established warehouse.

Speculation

The general rules of buying and selling precious metals just discussed are oriented toward those who buy gold and silver for the long-term. If you elect to speculate in precious metals by buying them for quick resale, you need to locate a good broker through whom you can buy and sell without paying the "normal" fees. Otherwise the short-term fluctuations will rarely cover the fees paid.

A second option is trading in futures on the commodities exchange. As I mentioned earlier, the only people I have personally known who were able to make money at it are the commodities brokers who live off of gullible amateur speculators. This type of investing is for the strong in heart and weak in mind (in my opinion).

20

Evaluating Insurance

I know of no investment subject that can generate as much emotion (on the part of salespeople) as that of insurance. For decades the insurance industry held a whole generation of potential investors captive to very low interest rates.

The reason the industry could do so is that people who lived through the Great Depression and saw their savings evaporate in banks, stocks, and virtually every other type of investment often lived off of the cash values in their insurance policies. They developed a well-earned trust of the insurance industry. For many it was the only store of money that survived the Depression. It mattered little that the interest rates they had earned were minuscule when compared to other investments.

After the Depression the insurance industry played off of this theme for decades, promoting the concept that only in insurance is an investor's money totally safe. For millions of Americans this was the gospel according to Prudential, or Metropolitan Life, or whomever.

The industry was quite effective in raising enormous amounts of capital, storing it in insurance policies, and paying about half of the going interest rates to their policy holders.

In the early seventies a new philosophy of insurance emerged: "buy term and invest the difference." The "term only" salesmen simply showed insurance clients how they could buy inexpensive term insurance, invest their savings in other products, primarily mutual funds, and profit greatly. This message reached a new generation who had not experienced the ravages of the Great Depression and were looking for earnings, not security. They bought into the concept of "buy term."

At first the insurance industry tried to ignore the "term" people. But as millions of "whole life" policies were dropped and converted over to term, the industry responded quickly. The result was a new generation of "whole life" products, such as universal life, minimum deposit life, and single premium life. These are actually modified whole life plans that offer higher rates of return for the savings portion of the policy.

In addition, the traditional insurance annuities, or retirement plans, were also upgraded to compete with the skyrocketing mutual fund industry.

In order to offer competitive returns to their policyholders, the insurance companies themselves had to become more competitive by investing their surplus capital at higher rates of return. After all, no company can pay out more than what they earn, at least not for long. As a result, many insurance companies now are faced with many high-risk investments—junk bonds, commercial loans, and commercial real estate—in their own portfolios.

It now behooves a prudent investor to evaluate carefully the insurance company that backs the policy he or she owns. An insurance company is a corporation (or an association). As such, the products they sell—life insurance, health insurance, annuities, etc.—are only as secure as the company itself.

In order to evaluate an investment in an insurance product, it is necessary to separate the insurance side from the investment side. A number of methods are commonly used to do this. One is to compare the cost of a term insurance policy with that of a whole life policy, less the "investment" side of the latter. The usual method is to use a 10- to 20-year comparison.

For example: Assume you purchased either a $100,000 annual renewable term policy for 30 years (age 35 to 65), or you purchased a $100,000 adjustable life plan at age 35. The adjustable life policy would cost $600 annually, and at age 65 would have accumulated approximately $10,000 in savings.

The annual renewable policy would cost $200 a year at age 35 and increase to $4,300 a year by age 65. Using the early years' savings on the term insurance to invest in a mutual fund averaging 10 percent annual growth, the net result at age 65 would be a loss of $3,700.

The difference in cost between term and whole life begins to narrow as the age increases, because the annual renewable policy gets progressively more expensive. The only way such a plan will work is to assume you can cancel the annual renewable insurance once your other sources of savings reach $100,000 (or at least reduce the coverage).

The bottom line is: If the total worth of the mutual fund at age 65 is greater than the total worth of the cash value policy, the term is a better investment. If not, the cash value insurance is better. In our example, the latter proved to be better.

This all may sound a little complicated, but any investment advisor or insurance agent with access to a computer can run this comparison for you in a few minutes.

Since I am not trying to sell you anything, I can tell you what I have observed. To date I have not seen any cash value insurance products (universal life, annuities, or other) that would match buying term insurance and investing the difference in a good quality growth mutual fund if the insured was able to shop for a new policy at least every three years. This continually allows for the lowest term rates. But with many of the newer whole life plans, such as adjustable life, the line between insurance and investment tends to blur.

I would also be less than totally honest if I didn't say that only a few people actually buy term and invest the difference. Most buy term and spend the difference. That's okay provided they consciously make that decision, but most simply fail to execute the plans they have made.

CASH VALUE POLICIES

The concept behind all cash value insurance policies is basically the same. The policy requires a fixed annual payment that is calculated to amortize the premiums as the insured gets older. By investing the early years' overcharge of premiums the insurance company can offset the costs in later years. Some of the newer plans called "minimum deposit" insurance require a set amount to be paid into the policy either as a lump sum or over the first few years. Then the deposit is invested and the proceeds are used to maintain the annual payments.

Some insurance companies are "stock companies" owned by investors. The policyholders have no ownership interest in the company. Normally stock companies pay lower returns to the policyholders because of the necessity to pay stockholder dividends, unlike "mutual" companies where each policyholder is a pro-rata owner in the company. In a mutual company, profits are distributed to the policyholders in the form of dividends.

Mutual companies were formed to compete directly with the older stock companies. They did so by passing along the profits to their policyholders. This arrangement increased the effective yield of the policies and attracted a large number of participants.

The actual yield to policyholders is often hard to discern because many companies, both mutual and stock, quote their gross yields before all commissions and expenses are taken out. Before investing in any insurance product you need to ask for a detailed analysis of *net* yield over the previous 10 years.

It is also important to remember that most quoted yields in insurance policies are projected only. They can be changed at any time because of prevailing market conditions, increased company expenses, and even investment losses by the company itself. The only dependable rate is the guaranteed rate, which is normally several percentage points lower than the projected rate.

If you decide to invest in an insurance product, you need to know what it will cost if you elect to drop the plan, withdraw your funds, switch plans, or stop paying any further. You also need to know what the annual fees are, including commissions.

One advantage of cash value insurance is that the cash value accumulation is not taxable to the insured. As noted earlier, this is because the cash values are really an overcharge of premiums and don't belong to the policy owner but to the insurance company. More recent policies do transfer ownership of the savings to the policy owners at specific intervals or upon the death of the insured.

ANNUITIES

There are basically two types of annuities: *fixed* and *variable*. The fixed annuities normally are offered as either single premium deferred or regular. Regular annuities are being used less and less because of their inflexibility. Once a payout has begun, the monthly payments cannot be changed.

A single premium deferred annuity operates much like a CD, except that the interest is not taxable until it is paid out (usually at age 59½ or later). The yield is normally higher than an equivalent CD. The deferred annuity is relatively liquid in that you can make penalty-free withdrawals of up to 10 percent a year of the accumulated interest.

I believe the variable annuity offers the most flexibility for investors under age 50. A variable annuity's return is based on its earnings, while a fixed annuity pays a guaranteed amount. Obviously there is a greater risk with a variable annuity. If the managers do well, so do the investors. If the managers do poorly, the investors lose too. But since a fixed annuity cannot be adjusted for inflation, it has little flexibility for younger investors.

I recommend that after age 60 any annuities be converted to a fixed payout. Most variable annuities offer this option.

QUESTIONS TO ASK ABOUT
INSURANCE AND ANNUITIES

1. *What year did the company begin operations?* A young company's operating ratios may look good, but keep in mind that a company less than 25 years old hasn't proved itself through a series of business cycles.

Another caution for investing in a young company is that the mortality rates may be inaccurate because it has not had the claims experience needed; that comes only through time.

2. *What is the company's form of corporation?* Insurance companies are under two major categories: mutual companies and stock companies. Mutual companies are owned by the policyholders, who share in the company's profits. Stock companies may direct all their earnings to shareholders or to a parent holding company. Mutual companies have historically been more inclined to provide better products for the consumer than stock companies.

3. *What company assets and insurance are in force?* Bigger isn't always or necessarily better, but a very small company may have difficulty in a period of adverse experience or may lack the expertise needed to handle a large case.

4. *How has the company fared with the rating services?* There are three main rating companies that rate insurance companies and financial institutions:

Moody's Investor's Service Incorporated assigns ratings based on a company's ability to discharge senior policyholders' obligations and claims. The ratings range from AAA (the highest) to C (the lowest). Categories are further divided by numerical modifiers from 1 to 3, with 1 being the highest. Moody's insurance rating is an *opinion* of the insurance company's ability to meet its policy obligations over a long-term period.

Standard and Poor's Corporation assigns each insurance company a rating which is an assessment of the company's ability to meet its obligations under the most adverse circumstances. The ratings range from AAA (the highest) to D (the lowest).

A.M. Best is an independent research service which publishes an annual review of insurance companies. Their overall ratings range from C (the lowest) to A+ (superior), and represent a company's financial solvency. Most consumer advocates recommend purchasing from an A+ rated company.

A.M. Best was started in 1905, Standard and Poor's in 1971, Moody's in 1986. A.M. Best rates over 1,400 U.S. companies; Standard and Poor's rates 110 companies; and Moody's, to this date, had rated 65 companies. It is extremely important to be aware of any changes in ratings. Information on these rating services is available in the Appendix.

5. *What are the company's operating ratios?* When evaluating a company's investment products, you need to be aware of the ratios that can help in determining the success of that company: mortality, net investment yield, lapse ratio, and renewal expense ratio. A company with better results in these areas is more likely to sustain favorable long-term returns.

Net yield is the overall return the company earned on its invested assets. The higher the number, the better the return. If a company says it is paying 10 percent, but you find that the company has only earned an 8 percent investment net yield, chances are it is going to be difficult to pay to the consumer a 10 percent return on that investment product.

Lapse ratio represents the amount of insurance terminated by lapse or surrender. High levels of lapse ratio usually mean increased expenses and may indicate customer dissatisfaction. Lower numbers mean less lapse activity and may indicate greater consumer satisfaction.

Mortality represents the dollar amount of claims the company paid in relation to the amount of insurance in force. A lower number means the company is experiencing better mortality costs and usually is an indication of quality underwriting.

Renewal expense ratio is a ratio of expenses to insurance in force and represents the operating efficiency of a company. A lower number means lower expenses.

Finally, in summary, look at exactly how the client has been treated after he is considered an old client. Many companies feel that old clients should be treated as fairly as new clients, which means that if there are substantial changes in new policies, the old policies are upgraded. This is extremely important because the day after you buy any product, you are an old client.

(NOTE: This information was provided courtesy of J.H. Shoemaker & Co., Inc., Memphis, Tennessee.)

21

Social Security and Estate Planning

S ince this is a book dealing with investments, not government welfare, I will limit my discussion to the retirement aspects of the Social Security system. If you would like to have more details on the other aspects of the Federal Insurance Contributions Act (FICA), otherwise known as Social Security, refer to the reference materials in the Appendix. The most thorough discussion I have read on this topic is *The Complete and Easy Guide to Social Security and Medicare* by Faustin Jehle. (See Appendix for another resource.)

I decided to include a separate section on Social Security retirement benefits because, like it or not, for the majority of Americans it is a forced "old age pension plan" that requires a substantial contribution from the day most of us go to work until we retire—or die. At present all covered workers are required to "contribute" over 15½ percent of their wages up to $53,400 a year. It is an absolute certainty that both the percentage and the maximum salary to be taxed will increase during the next decade as more "baby boomers" retire.

Many salaried employees do not realize that the total FICA tax is over 15 percent because the portion an employee must pay is one-half of the total tax. But I assure you that the portion paid by an employer is a part of an employee's salary and directly affects what an employer can pay in total salary.

Social Security does have some good benefits, especially for those people who would never discipline themselves to put anything aside for later years. But actually it is a bad investment, as far as retirement benefits go. For someone who began working in 1960 at age 25, and paid into the system for the next 42 years until age 67 (the retirement age for workers born since 1938), the contributions they made to Social Security (assuming they started at the 50 percent of maximum level and went to 100 percent in 10 years) would yield a retirement income of approximately $20,000 a year. The same amount of investment in an annuity that earned 6 percent (tax deferred) would pay over $60,000 a year at age 67! And the income from the annuity would not be affected by additional outside earnings, as Social Security benefits are.

But since contributions to the system are no longer "voluntary," you do need to understand how the system functions and what you can expect to receive at retirement age. For those workers born before 1938, the retirement age is 65 for 100 percent benefits. Social Security offers the option to retire as early as age 62 (disabled workers are subject to more lenient rules). Those who elect to retire at age 62 have their retirement benefits reduced by 20 percent.

If you retire at any time before age 65, your benefits are reduced by 0.555 times the number of months before retirement age. For instance, if you retire 30 months early, your formula would be 30 x 0.555 = 16.65%. So your benefits would be reduced by 16.65 percent a year.

To take a 20-percent reduction in lifetime benefits by retiring at 62 may sound like a bad option. But since you would receive 36 monthly checks prior to 65 it would take nearly 12 years of earnings at the higher rate to break even. So in great part it depends on your long-range goals.

GET AN AUDIT

Since the earnings you make during your working career directly affect the amount you will earn upon retirement, it is important to calculate what your benefits will be for planning purposes. This is particularly true for those over age 50.

A worker is deemed to be fully "vested" or insured once he has paid into the system for 40 quarters, with some exceptions made for those who came into the system as a result of tax law changes passed in 1984. However, since the government never makes anything simple, there are several exceptions. A quarter for Social Security purposes is also any period in which a worker earns the required amount ($540 as of 1991). So if you were paid $2,160 for any month that year, you earned four quarters worth of credit ($540 x 4 = $2,160), but you cannot accumulate more than four quarters of Social Security benefits in a single year, no matter how much you earned.

The schedule for minimum annual earnings has been increased as the Social Security tax and benefits have increased, so earlier years require less earnings, later years more.

Also, retirement benefits are adjusted for different levels of earnings, so participation in later years can enhance earnings, while nonparticipation will reduce retirement earnings.

If the accuracy of the Social Security Administration equals that of other branches of the federal government, you can expect some errors in your records. Many people have been shocked to find out that their benefits have been miscalculated due to contributions not being allocated to their accounts properly. It is important to audit your Social Security file prior to retirement so that you can clear up any errors if necessary. The Social Security Administration will run a free audit of your file upon request. This form is the "Request for Earnings and Benefits Statement." You can obtain one at no cost by calling your local Social Security office and requesting a copy of Form SSA-7004PC [see Figure 1, p. 234]. Once you fill this out and return it, the audit normally follows in six to eight weeks, and is called the "Personal Earnings and Benefit Record" (Form SSA-700PC).

After you receive the audit of your work record (and your spouse's too), you will need to review it carefully. It will show

SOCIAL SECURITY ADMINISTRATION

Request for Earnings and Benefit Estimate Statement

To receive a free statement of your earnings covered by Social Security and your estimated future benefits, all you need to do is fill out this form. Please print or type your answers. When you have completed the form, fold it and mail it to us.

1. Name shown on your Social Security card:

First ___ Middle Initial ___ Last

2. Your Social Security number as shown on your card:
☐☐☐ - ☐☐ - ☐☐☐☐

3. Your date of birth: Month ___ Day ___ Year

4. Other Social Security numbers you may have used:
☐☐☐ - ☐☐ - ☐☐☐☐
☐☐☐ - ☐☐ - ☐☐☐☐

5. Your Sex: ☐ Male ☐ Female

6. Other names you have used (including a maiden name):

7. Show your actual earnings for last year and your estimated earnings for this year. Include only wages and/or net self-employment income subject to Social Security tax.

A. Last year's actual earnings:
$ ☐☐☐,☐☐☐.☐☐
Dollars only

B. This year's estimated earnings:
$ ☐☐☐,☐☐☐.☐☐
Dollars only

8. Show the age at which you plan to retire:

9. Below, show an amount which you think best represents your future average yearly earnings between now and when you plan to retire. The amount should be a yearly average, not your total future lifetime earnings. Only show earnings subject to Social Security tax.

Most people should enter the same amount as this year's estimated earnings (the amount shown in 7B). The reason for this is that we will show your retirement benefit estimate in today's dollars, but adjusted to account for average wage growth in the national economy.

However, if you expect to earn significantly more or less in the future than what you currently earn because of promotions, a job change, part-time work, or an absence from the work force, enter the amount in today's dollars that will most closely reflect your future average yearly earnings. Do not add in cost-of-living, performance, or scheduled pay increases or bonuses.

Your future average yearly earnings:
$ ☐☐☐,☐☐☐.☐ 0 0
Dollars only

10. Address where you want us to send the statement:

Name ___

Street Address (include Apt. No., P.O. Box, or Rural Route) ___

City ___ State ___ Zip Code ___

I am asking for information about my own Social Security record or the record of a person I am authorized to represent. I understand that if I deliberately request information under false pretenses I may be guilty of a federal crime and/or jailed and/or imprisoned. I authorize you to send the statement of my earnings and benefit estimates to me or my representative through a contractor.

Please sign your name (Do not print)

▲ ___

Date ___ (Area Code) Daytime Telephone No.

ABOUT THE PRIVACY ACT
Social Security is allowed to collect the facts on this form under Section 205 of the Social Security Act. We need them to quickly identify your record and prepare the earnings statement you asked us for. Giving us these facts is voluntary. However, without them we may not be able to give you an earnings and benefit estimate statement. Neither the Social Security Administration nor its contractor will use the information for any other purpose.

SP ☐

Form SSA-7004-PC-OP1 (6/88) DESTROY PRIOR EDITIONS

Figure 1.

every year in which you were credited for contributions and how many credits you have earned. It will also provide an estimate of your projected retirement benefits (plus disability and survivor's benefits) and the amount by which your benefits would be reduced for early retirement [see Figure 2, p. 236-37]. This is an excellent service provided by the Social Security Administration and you should take advantage of it.

By the way, a 1987 study done by the Government Accounting Office (GAO) estimated that as many as 9 million American workers may have errors in their work records. So check it out! If you find that your file has errors, you will need to appeal to the Social Security Administration for correction. Finding the W-2s or similar records for past years may not be simple. If you have not kept them, you will need to appeal to the IRS for copies (good luck).

SURVIVOR BENEFITS

In doing your retirement planning it is important to factor in the survivor's benefits. I will assume for illustration purposes that the husband was fully insured for maximum benefits and chose to retire at age 65 (67 for those born after 1938. In the event the insured worker dies, the spouse is entitled to only 50 percent of his or her benefits (except in the case of disability or dependent children). Failure to compensate for this reduction can result in financial hardship for the spouse.

The best way to plan around this problem is to store enough assets to provide for you both with only 50 percent of Social Security benefits available. That way the transition will be painless for the surviving spouse. Since your source of income is unearned (as opposed to wages), the additional income will not affect your Social Security benefits under present laws.

Once your budget is established on 50-percent Social Security income, you can reinvest the additional Social Security as a hedge against inflation or premature death or you can give it to the Lord's work.

TABLE FOR ESTIMATING AMOUNTS OF SOCIAL SECURITY BENEFITS

Average Monthly Wage	Old-Age Benefit Age 65	Old-Age Benefit Age 62	Dependent Spouse Age 65	Dependent Spouse Age 62	Average Monthly Wage	Old-Age Benefit Age 65	Old-Age Benefit Age 62	Dependent Spouse Age 65	Dependent Spouse Age 62	Average Monthly Wage	Old-Age Benefit Age 65	Old-Age Benefit Age 62	Dependent Spouse Age 65	Dependent Spouse Age 62
$83	144	115	72	54	609	495	396	248	186	1250	710	568	355	266
92	158	127	79	59	641	517	413	258	194	1275	716	573	358	269
101	172	138	86	65	660	527	421	263	198	1300	722	578	361	271
107	184	147	92	69	685	536	429	268	201	1325	729	583	364	273
122	195	156	105	79	705	544	435	272	204	1350	735	588	367	276
146	210	168	105	79	725	551	441	276	207	1375	741	593	371	278
169	224	179	112	84	745	559	447	280	210	1400	747	597	373	280
193	239	191	119	90	770	567	454	284	213	1425	753	602	376	282
216	253	202	127	95	790	573	459	287	215	1450	759	607	379	285
239	268	215	134	101	810	580	464	290	218	1475	764	612	382	287
258	280	224	140	105	835	588	470	294	221	1500	770	616	385	289
281	294	235	147	110	860	596	477	298	223	1525	775	620	388	291
300	306	245	153	115	885	604	483	302	226	1550	781	625	390	293
323	320	256	160	120	910	611	489	306	229	1575	786	629	393	295
342	331	265	166	124	930	618	494	309	232	1600	792	635	396	297
365	346	277	173	130	955	626	501	313	235	1625	797	638	399	299
389	361	288	180	135	980	634	507	317	238	1650	803	642	401	301

Figure 2.

236

TABLE FOR ESTIMATING AMOUNTS OF SOCIAL SECURITY BENEFITS

Average Monthly Wage	Old-Age Benefit Age 65	Old-Age Benefit Age 62	Dependent Spouse Age 65	Dependent Spouse Age 62
412	375	300	188	141
436	388	311	194	146
459	402	322	201	151
478	413	330	206	155
501	427	341	213	160
524	440	352	220	165
548	454	363	227	170
563	464	371	232	174
577	473	379	237	178
591	483	387	242	181

Average Monthly Wage	Old-Age Benefit Age 65	Old-Age Benefit Age 62	Dependent Spouse Age 65	Dependent Spouse Age 62
1000	640	512	320	240
1030	648	519	324	243
1050	654	523	327	245
1075	661	529	331	248
1100	669	535	334	251
1125	676	540	338	253
1150	683	546	341	256
1175	690	552	345	259
1200	696	557	348	261
1225	703	562	352	264

Average Monthly Wage	Old-Age Benefit Age 65	Old-Age Benefit Age 62	Dependent Spouse Age 65	Dependent Spouse Age 62
1675	808	647	404	303
1700	814	651	407	305
1725	819	655	410	307
1750	825	660	412	309
1775	830	664	415	311
1800	836	669	418	313
1825	841	673	421	315
1850	847	677	423	318
1875	852	682	426	320
1900	858	686	429	322

MEDICARE HEALTH BENEFITS

Perhaps the greatest current benefit of the Social Security program is health care for older Americans. I almost hesitate to comment on this feature because I am totally convinced that, except for retirees before the end of this century, the program will be greatly modified to eliminate many current benefits. Sadly, it is a great idea that is simply too expensive to survive long-term unless the government also goes into the health care business to control costs. And how would you like to go to a government hospital to qualify for Medicare benefits? One thing is for sure, the morbidity rate would lower the number of Social Security retirees drastically!

It is my opinion that the trend in Medicare will be similar to that of the Medicaid program provided by the states. The Medicaid benefit is available by need only, and access to the system is limited to the indigent. If Medicare does evolve in this direction, the very planning that prudent investors do will work against them because it serves to build a strong asset base.

Assuming that Medicare does restructure to provide health care benefits only to the indigent, there is a possible alternative available. You can join with a group of similarly minded people of all ages who can provide the funds necessary to care for the older retirees. These are called "associations" and, in fact, there are at least two in operation now that I know of and more that are sure to develop as health care costs escalate. The concept is simple and is based on the principle taught in 2 Corinthians 8:14-15:

> At this present time your abundance being a supply for their want, that their abundance also may become a supply for your want, that there may be equality; as it is written, "He who gathered much did not have too much, and he who gathered little had no lack."

Virtually every insurance company is founded upon this

principle: that there are more healthy people than sick, and the healthy can pool their resources to care for the sick, knowing that when they are ill, others will do the same for them.

Two groups that practice this concept are listed in the Appendix under "Health Care Alternatives." At the time of this writing the cost of an average family health care insurance plan is about $300 per month nationwide. The cost per family in these associations is only about $110 per month, primarily because the groups are comprised of nondrinkers and nonsmokers, and coverage is limited to major expenses related to hospital stays. Also, since each member has a vested interest in keeping costs down, there is an active effort to monitor and limit all excessive bills.

To my knowledge there is no other health care resource available that will provide as much coverage for so little cost. Normally even a Medicare supplement will cost that much, or more.

ESTATE INFORMATION

Since a portion of anyone's long-range financial planning must be balanced with the inevitability of death, it is important to plan for that eventuality as well. If you do no planning for what happens upon your death, the effects can be devastating on your survivors, especially your spouse. As stewards of the Lord's resources, it is not an option to ignore the inevitable. Indeed, it is the height of selfishness for a provider to ignore the needs of his or her dependents after death.

The minimum planning anyone should do is to have a current, valid will while living. A well-drafted will directs how the assets should be distributed upon the owner's death. Both husband and wife need wills in the event they are killed in a common accident. In larger estates, the tax consequences of estate assets passing from husband to wife to heirs in a concurrent death situation can severely dilute an estate. With no wills, the certainty is that the state is going to assume the worst case situation; that is, to their financial benefit.

A simple will (as of this writing) can cost as little as $100, depending on the attorney involved. The more complex the estate situation, the higher the costs can run. It is always important to locate the most knowledgeable attorney, even at a somewhat higher cost. The only time you need a will is after you die. If the attorney made a mistake, it's too late to correct it then.

ESTATE TAXES

The current federal estate tax law allows for an unlimited amount of assets to be passed along to a surviving spouse, and approximately $600,000 to other heirs, without incurring any federal estate tax. In larger estates it is important that the ownership and assignment of assets be carefully checked by someone knowledgeable in estate planning. For instance, insurance proceeds that are assigned to a surviving spouse as beneficiary become taxable estate assets upon the death of the second spouse. If the insurance is assigned to a trust with the surviving spouse receiving lifetime income benefits, the tax consequences can be greatly reduced.

The federal estate taxes begin (presently) at 37 percent on estates above $600,000 and go to 55 percent [see Figure 3, p. 241], so they are not inconsequential for larger estates. It would be a shame to allow your hard-earned assets to be allocated to the government when, with a simple will or trust, they could go into God's work.

STATE DEATH TAXES

Most states use the federal estate tax codes as their guide for state death taxes, but not all. These exceptions can be disastrous if you don't know about them. Figure 4 (p. 242) shows the taxes per state as of this writing. Obviously these can and do change if state laws change. I would heartily encourage you

Unified Rate Schedule for Estates and Gift Taxes			
If the Amount Is		Tentative Tax Is	On Excess Amount Over
Over This	But Not Over		
$ 0	$ 10,000	0 plus 18%	$ 0
10,000	20,000	1,800 plus 20%	10,000
20,000	40,000	3,800 plus 22%	20,000
40,000	60,000	8,200 plus 24%	40,000
60,000	80,000	13,000 plus 26%	60,000
80,000	100,000	18,200 plus 28%	80,000
100,000	150,000	23,800 plus 30%	100,000
150,000	250,000	38,800 plus 32%	150,000
250,000	500,000	70,800 plus 34%	250,000
500,000	750,000	155,800 plus 37%	500,000
750,000	1,000,000	248,300 plus 39%	750,000
1,000,000	1,250,000	345,800 plus 41%	1,000,000
1,250,000	1,500,000	448,300 plus 43%	1,250,000
1,500,000	2,000,000	555,800 plus 45%	1,500,000
2,000,000	2,500,000	780,800 plus 49%	2,000,000
2,500,000	3,000,000	1,025,800 plus 53%	2,500,000
3,000,000	10,000,000	1,290,800 plus 55%	3,000,000
10,000,000	21,040,000	5,140,800 plus 60%	10,000,000
21,040,000	....	11,764,800 plus 55%	21,040,000

Figure 3.

to contact a good estate planning attorney to verify the tax consequences in your state.

PROBATE COSTS

A number of books currently give much attention to how to avoid probate costs. This in turn has sparked an interest in the

State	Death tax ($) On $600,000 estate left to: Spouse	Child	State	Death tax ($) On $600,000 estate left to: Spouse	Child	State	Death tax ($) On $600,000 estate left to: Spouse	Child
Alabama	None	None	Louisiana	$17,050	$17,050	Ohio	$2,100	$30,100
Arizona	None	None	Maine	None	None	Oklahoma	0	17,725
Arkansas	None	None	Maryland	6,000	6,000	Oregon	None	None
California	None	None	Massachusetts	23,500	55,500	Pennsylvania	36,000	36,000
Colorado	None	None	Michigan	0	33,700	Rhode Island	7,900	12,400
Connecticut	$0	$37,875	Minnesota	None	None	South Carolina	0	33,000
Delaware	0	31,250	Mississippi	0	1,400	South Dakota	0	41,250
Dist. of Columbia	None	None	Missouri	None	None	Tennessee	0	0
Florida	None	None	Montana	0	0	Texas	None	None
Georgia	None	None	Nebraska	0	5,850	Utah	None	None
Hawaii	None	None	Nevada	None	None	Vermont	None	None
Idaho	None	None	New Hampshire	0	0	Virginia	None	None
Illinois	None	None	New Jersey	0	0	Washington	None	None
Indiana	0	24,950	New Mexico	None	None	West Virginia	None	None
Iowa	0	39,825	New York	25,500	25,500	Wisconsin	0	56,250
Kansas	0	21,750	North Carolina	0	7,000	Wyoming	None	None
Kentucky	0	45,370	North Dakota	None	None			

Figure 4.

use of trusts to avoid these costs. Many valid reasons exist why someone would need a trust but, in most instances, probate is not one of them.

In most states the cost of probating (proving) an in-state

will is nominal. I live in Georgia, where the probate cost is about $50. A trust to avoid this expense would cost significantly more, and the ownership of all assets must also be changed to assign them to the trust. I am not trying to discourage anyone from using a trust if their attorney advises, but be certain of the costs and savings first. Obviously the probate cost in some states is more significant. In fact, many elderly people move from high-cost states to those with lower costs just to spare their estate the expense. Check with the court of the ordinary in your community to determine the probate costs in your state.

THE USE OF TRUSTS

Several excellent books on wills and trusts are listed in the Appendix, so I won't even attempt to elaborate on this issue, especially since I am not an attorney and would simply be drawing from what I had read in those publications. What I would like to do is at least acquaint you with the basics of using trusts so that you can factor that information into your long-range strategy.

There are two basic types of trusts: living (inter-vivos), and dead (testamentary). These can be further divided into two additional categories: revocable and irrevocable. The first you can change while you are still living. The second you cannot. Obviously a living, revocable trust becomes a testamentary, irrevocable trust upon the death of the person involved.

Assets assigned to a living, revocable trust are still a part of the owner's estate, and the assets assigned to that trust will be subject to estate and death taxes, but not probate costs.

Assets placed in an irrevocable trust are no longer a part of the grantor's (owner's) estate and can avoid estate taxes if the trust is qualified. Obviously they would also avoid probate, since a trust does not require probating.

A testamentary trust is one created by the death of the grantor, usually within a will. The assets are assigned to the trust upon the completion of probate and the trust controls the assets from that point on. It is common for one spouse to create a trust within the couple's will that will provide for the care of the other spouse during his or her lifetime, with the assets going elsewhere upon the death of the surviving spouse. By doing so, a portion of the estate and death taxes can be avoided.

OTHER TRUSTS

There is a proliferation of other specialized trusts at the disposal of qualified estate-planning attorneys. Among them are many charitable trusts that provide current tax-saving benefits and allow the ultimate disposition of the assets to go to the qualified charity of your choice. I have known many Christians who have used charitable trusts to provide for their loved ones, save taxes, and fund the Lord's work. Any of the books listed in the Appendix discuss these trusts also.

QUESTIONS AND ANSWERS

Because of the many questions raised by such a brief discussion of such a complex subject, I thought that a short question-and-answer section would help to clarify some of them. I would always add this disclaimer: I am not an attorney, nor an estate planner. Before acting on any of the information in this section, consult with your own attorney.

Question 1: *Can I draft my own will without having to pay an attorney?*

Answer: Yes, you can in the majority of states. A self-drawn will is called a holographic will. Holographic means that it is a document written totally in the handwriting of the person drafting it. The rules governing holographic wills vary by state, and you must thoroughly understand the laws of your state to ensure your will is probatable (provable) in court.

Question 2: *What if one of my witnesses has died?*

Answer: In order for a will to be probated, the judge may require the will to be verified. If you used only two witnesses and the state requires a minimum of two, both must be alive and available. It is always best to use three or even four witnesses that you know well. If less than the required minimum are still alive, you will need to amend your will with a codicil to have other witnesses verify it.

Question 3: *Should I keep my will in a safety deposit box?*

Answer: If you do so, you need to be sure that someone else has access to the box. Since a safety deposit box cannot be opened except by court order, the process can be lengthy and expensive in the event of your death. If no one else knows about the box, it may never be recovered. I suggest that you name your spouse as an authorized signatory, as well as your attorney or accountant.

Question 4: *Do I need a new will if I change residences from one state to another?*

Answer: Possibly. You need to have an attorney in the new state review your will to ensure it conforms to that state's laws.

Question 5: *What if I own property in more than one state?*

Answer: Generally, your estate is governed by the state in which you reside at the time of your death. Thus a valid will drawn in your state can control the distribution of assets in another state, even if that state's laws are different.

Question 6: *Do I need a will if my wife and I hold all of our property in joint tenancy?*

Answer: Yes. Joint tenancy means that the surviving tenant or spouse owns the property upon the death of the other tenant, but if there are assets owned outside the joint properties, they would not be covered. In our generation this is common where there may be large settlements due to negligent deaths, such as an automobile accident.

Bear in mind also that some states tax joint property as if the deceased owned it outright, while others tax a proportionate interest in it. You will need to check with an attorney in your state to determine how jointly owned properties are taxed, if at all.

Also, if both of you are killed in a common accident, the last surviving tenant would be declared intestate (without a valid will). The estate would be subject to dual taxation and additional legal costs.

Question 7: *Who can I name as my estate executor?*

Answer: You can name anyone you desire to act as executor of your will and estate. That person's duties are to probate the will and distribute the assets accordingly. You may choose to name more than one person to serve as executor and should always name at least three alternates in the event that one cannot or will not serve.

Unless you stipulate otherwise, many states require an out-of-state executor to post a bond. Some require a bond equal to the value of the estate. Since your estate will have to bear this cost, you may want to waive the requirement to post bond.

Bear in mind that if you use a professional executor, a fee will be charged. This can vary from an hourly fee to a percentage of the estate value. Any such fees should be clearly spelled out in a contract and attached to your will or trust.

Question 8: *What is a trust?*

Answer: A trust is a legal contract to manage someone's assets before and/or after death. There are two basic types of trusts: a "living" trust, known as an inter-vivos trust, and a "testamentary" trust, meaning that it commences upon the death of the person.

Question 9: *What is the advantage of a trust?*

Answer: A trust is not a public document, as is a will, and does not require probate. Thus, a trust ensures a greater measure of privacy. Also, since a trust is not probatable, there are no probate costs associated with assets held in a living trust. Since a testamentary trust is created within a will (normally), the will must first be probated before the trust becomes effective. A testamentary trust therefore does not avoid probate costs on the assets of the assignee.

If the living trust is irrevocable, the assets held in trust are not subject to estate taxes, except to the extent that the assignee retains an interest in them. Literally, the assets are given to trust and become trust property. There may be gift taxes due on assets assigned to a trust for the benefit of others.

Question 10: *Can I draft my own trust?*

Answer: Will and trust "kits" are available in most bookstores today. These purport to explain how to draft your own will or simple trust. While it is legal for a layman to draft a holographic will or trust, I personally don't advise it. Once you are deceased, it's too late to change the will or trust if it doesn't pass the test. As the old saying goes, you can be "penny wise and pound foolish."

Question 11: *How much tax will my estate have to pay?*

Answer: That depends on the value of your estate at death. Through a marital deduction allowance, each spouse can leave the other an unlimited amount of assets. However, assets left to someone other than a spouse are subject to estate (death) taxes. (See the section on federal and state estate taxes earlier in this chapter.)

Question 12: *When are the taxes due?*

Answer: Usually within six months of death, the state will require an appraisal of the estate. The taxes are due and payable at that time, although in practice both the state and federal tax collectors will normally work out a plan to convert the assets necessary to pay the taxes so that the estate doesn't suffer a severe dilution through a forced sale.

Liquidity (cash) in an estate is very important since the taxes must be paid in cash. Otherwise, assets must be sold to satisfy the tax collectors. If the assets cannot be sold through normal market channels, the estate may be auctioned off at a substantial loss.

Question 13: *What if I change my mind after I make a will?*

Answer: You can change your will through the use of a codicil (supplement). The codicil is subject to the same laws of probate, so it is important that it be drafted properly. Attach all codicils to the original will and store them together. Remember that only the original will or codicil is probatable, so protect them carefully.

Appendix

Guide to Appendix Information

(The information and advice provided by these resources do not necessarily represent the opinions of the publisher or the author.)

GUIDES TO BUYING ANTIQUES

(1) *Antiques and Collectibles Price Guide*
Katherine Murphy
Dubuque, IA: Babka Publishing Co., 1986

(2) *Emyl Jenkins' Appraisal Book*
Emyl Jenkins
New York, NY: Crown Publishing, Inc., 1989

ASSET MANAGEMENT SERVICES

(1) Pryor & Associates
2337 Glen Eagle Drive
Louisville, KY 40222

(2) Winrich Capital Management, Inc.
23702 Birtcher Drive
Lake Forest, CA 92630

RARE COIN RATINGS/APPRAISALS

(1) The American Numismatic Association (ANA)
Certification Service
818 N. Cascade Avenue
Colorado Springs, CO 80903

(2) Certified Coin Dealer Newsletter
P.O. Box 11099
Torrance, CA 90510

(subscription fee; published weekly)

(3) *A Guide Book of United States Coins*
R.S. Yeoman
Racine, WI: Western Publishing

(published annually)

(4) Numismatic Guarantee Corporation of America
P.O. Box 1776
Parsippany, NJ 07054

(5) Professional Coin Grading Service (PCGS)
P.O. Box 9458
Newport Beach, CA 92658

PRECIOUS GEMS SERVICES

(1) American Gemological Laboratory
12th Floor
580 Fifth Avenue
New York, NY 10036

(2) National Gem Appraising Laboratory
8600 Fenton Street
Silver Spring, MD 20910

(3) United States Gemological Services
No. 237
14801 Yorba Street
Tustin, CA 92680

GOLD AND SILVER SERVICES

(1) The Silver and Gold Report
P.O. Box 2923
West Palm Beach, FL 33402

(subscription fee)

ALTERNATE HEALTH CARE SERVICES

(1) The Good Samaritan
P.O. Box 279
Beech Grove, IN 46107

317/783-7080 or
317/787-9770

(2) Brotherhood Newsletter
P.O. Box 832
Barberton, OH 44203
216/848-1511

INSURANCE COMPANY
RATING SERVICES

(1) A.M. Best Company
Ambest Road
Oldwick, NJ 08858-9999

(2) Duff & Phelps Inc.
Suite 3600
55 E. Monroe Street
Chicago, IL 60603

(3) Moody's Investor Service Incorporated
99 Church Street
New York, NY 10007-2787

(4) Standard & Poor's Corporation
25 Broadway
New York, NY 10004-1064

MUTUAL FUND MARKET TIMING

(1) Telephone Switch Newsletter
P.O. Box 2538
Huntington Beach, CA 92647

(subscription fee)

MUTUAL FUND SERVICES

(1) Guide to Mutual Funds
Investment Company Institute
1600 M Street, N.W.
Washington, DC 20036

(fees for material)

(2) Income and Safety
Institute of Econometric Research
3471 N. Federal Highway
Fort Lauderdale, FL 33306

(subscription fee)

(3) Mutual Fund Education Alliance
The Association of No-Load Funds
520 N. Michigan Avenue
Suite 1632
Chicago, IL 60611

(fees for material)

(4) Mutual Fund Forecaster
Institute of Econometric Research
3471 N. Federal Highway
Fort Lauderdale, FL 33306

(subscription fee)

(5) Mutual Fund Values Newsletter
Morningstar, Inc.
53 W. Jackson Boulevard
Chicago, IL 60604

(subscription fee)

(6) No-Load Fund-X
235 Montgomery Street
San Francisco, CA 94104

(subscription fee)

(7) Sound Mind Investing Newsletter
2337 Glen Eagle Drive
Louisville, KY 40222

(subscription fee)

FINANCIAL NEWSLETTER
RATING SERVICES

(1) The Hulbert Guide to Financial Newsletters
Mark Hulbert
In Association with Minerva Books (Alexandria, VA)
Probus Publishing Company
1925 N. Clybourn Avenue
Chicago, IL 60614
312/868-1100

(subscription fee)

GENERAL FINANCIAL NEWSLETTERS

(1) The Cornerstone Investment Newsletter
Suite 301
297 Herndon Parkway
Herndon, VA 22070

(subscription fee)

(2) Financial Perspective
1600 N.W. 2nd Avenue
Suite 217
Boca Raton, FL 33432

(subscription fee)

(3) Good Money: The Newsletter for Socially Concerned Investors
Good Money Publications, Inc.
Box 363
Worcester, VT 05682

(subscription fee)

(4) Lynch Municipal Bond Advisory, Inc.
P.O. Box 25114
Santa Fe, NM 87504

(subscription fee)

(5) The McAlvany Intelligence Advisor
   P.O. Box 84904
   Phoenix, AZ 85071

   (subscription fee)

(6) The Money Strategy Letter
   P.O. Box 4130
   Medford, OR 97501

   (subscription fee)

(7) The Social Investment Forum
   711 Atlantic Avenue
   Boston, MA 12111

   (subscription fee)

TAX-DEFERRED RETIREMENT PLANS

(1) IRA
(2) SEP IRA
(3) SARSEP
(4) 401-K
(5) Tax Sheltered Annuity (403-B)
(6) HR-10 (Keogh)
(7) Pension
(8) Profit Sharing

Contact your tax or investment advisor for specific details on these plans.

SOCIAL SECURITY GUIDES

(1) *The Complete and Easy Guide to Social Security and Medicare*
   Faustin Jehle
   Fraser Inc.
   Box 1507
   Madison, CT 06443

(2) *What You Should Know about Your Social Security Now*
The Research Institute of America, Inc.
589 5th Avenue
New York, NY 10017

(a free publication)

STAMP COLLECTING SERVICES

(1) The American Philatelic Society
P.O. Box 8000
State College, PA 16801

(2) The Collector's Club
22 East 35th Street
New York, NY 10016

STOCK SERVICES

(1) The Dick Davis Digest
P.O. Box 9547
Fort Lauderdale, FL 33310-9547

(subscription fee)

(2) The Value Line Investment Survey
711 Third Avenue
New York, NY 10017

(subscription fee)

RESOURCE MATERIALS ON WILLS AND TRUSTS

(1) *Family Guide to Estate Planning*
Theodore E. Hughes
Scribner

(2) *A Second Start: A Widow's Guide to Financial Survival*
Judith N. Brown/Christina Baldwin
Simon & Schuster

(3) *Plan Your Estate with a Living Trust* and *Nolo's Simple Will Book*
Denis Clifford
Nolo Press

(4) *Thy Will Be Done: A Guide to Wills, Estates, and Taxation for Older People*
Eugene Daly
Prometheus Books

(5) *The Essential Guide to Wills, Estates, Trusts, and Death Taxes*
Alex J. Soled
Scott, Foresman, Lifelong Learning Division

RECOMMENDED READING

(1) *Encyclopedia of Investments*
Jack P. Friedmon
Warren, Gorham & Lamont

(2) *One Up on Wall Street: How to Use What You Already Know to Make Money in the Market*
Peter Lynch
Simon & Schuster (hardback); Viking Penguin (paperback)

(3) *Personal Financial Planning*
G. Victor Hallman & Jerry S. Rosenbloom
McGraw-Hill Book Co.

(4) *The Templeton Plan: 21 Steps to Personal Success and Real Happiness*
James Ellison
Harper & Row

(5) *The Thoughtful Christian's Guide to Investing*
Gary Moore
Zondervan Books

(6) *Your Finances in Changing Times*
Larry Burkett
Moody Press

(7) *The Complete Financial Guide for Young Couples*
Larry Burkett
Victor Books

(8) *The Complete Financial Guide for Single Parents*
Larry Burkett
Victor Books

RESOURCE CONTRIBUTORS

(1) Thomas G. Cloud
Cloud & Associates Consulting, Inc.
8735 Dunwoody Place
Suite O
Atlanta, GA 30350

(2) Kenneth Frenke, CFP
1600 N.W. 2nd Avenue
Suite 217
Boca Raton, FL 33432

(3) George M. Hiller, JD, LLM, MBA, CFP
Wealth Management
1800 Peachtree Street, N.W.
Suite 200
Atlanta, GA 30309

(4) Greg Holloway
The Continental Investment Group, Inc.
10000 North Central
Suite 1040
Dallas, TX 75231

(5) Faustin Jehle
c/o Fraser Inc.
Box 1507
Madison, CT 06443

(6) Vernon D. "Woody" Laywell
Laywell Financial Services
14702 Carolcrest
Houston, TX 77079

(7) Don McAlvany
International Collectors Associates
First Colorado Bank & Trust
2969 S. Colorado Boulevard
Suite 430
Denver, CO 80222

(8) Dr. James McKeever
P.O. Box 4130
Medford, OR 97501

(9) Austin Pryor
Pryor & Associates
2337 Glen Eagle Drive
Louisville, KY 40222

(10) Robert R. Rhinehart
Merrill Lynch
3500 Piedmont Road, N.E.
Suite 600
Atlanta, GA 30305

(11) Bill Robertson, CLU, CFP, ChFC
William F. Robertson & Associates
1200 Summit Avenue
Suite 516
Fort Worth, TX 76102

(12) James H. Shoemaker, CLU, CFP, ChFC
J. H. Shoemaker & Co.
58 Timber Creek Drive
Cordova, TN 38018

(13) Winrich Capital Management, Inc.
23702 Birtcher Drive
Lake Forest, CA 92630